4,95

Dying into Life

Dying into Life

A Study in Christian Life Styles

Pierce Johnson

ABINGDON PRESS
Nashville and New York

DYING INTO LIFE

ISBN: 0-687-11279-6

Library of Congress Catalog Card Number: 72-186828

Scripture quotations unless otherwise noted are from the
Revised Standard Version of the Bible, copyrighted 1946 and
1952 by the Division of Christian Education, National
Council of Churches, and are used by permission.

Quotations from *Markings*, by Dag Hammarskjöld, trans. by Leif Sjoberg
and W. H. Auden, copyright © 1964 by Alfred A. Knopf, Inc. and Faber
and Faber, Ltd. Reprinted by permission of Alfred A. Knopf, Inc.

MANUFACTURED BY THE PARTHENON PRESS AT
NASHVILLE, TENNESSEE, UNITED STATES OF AMERICA

To
Nancy Crandall Johnson, my wife,
the one with whom I do my dying and rising,
to Nancy, most of all for her courage
in carrying the constant cross of love and care,
to her most personally of all
I dedicate this book

Acknowledgments

"Dying into life" has been the dominant theme in my thought for over twenty years. As a Methodist minister and in my doctoral dissertation I have explored this theme in my own experience, in the churches I have served, and in my study of the archetypes of Christian history. To those with whom I have shared this search I am grateful.

Delia Clayton, my saintly "Aunt Delia," who always witnessed to the life of Christian humility, I do not forget. Nor Dixon and Julia Oberdorfer in their life of forgiveness and compassion.

Georgia Harkness is the person to whom I am most indebted in the writing of this book. She first urged me to write, and then she carefully and critically read every paragraph and page, week by week and month by month, as the study took shape. Known as "the teacher to Methodism," she has been my teacher too. No one could have been a better critic and teacher and friend than Georgia.

John B. Cobb, Jr., is the modern theologian who most commands my respect, and to him I am grateful for his reading of the manuscript and for revolutionary suggestions that turn me around, both in this study and in our friendship across the years.

Hans Dieter Betz read the chapter on Paul, and with his criticism I can be confident that I have learned my lessons in his classes and from his pioneering new understanding of the New Testament.

The Claremont United Methodist Church in Claremont, California, has been the life-giving community in which I have lived and out of which I have written. Here I would remember the communion of my saints.

Contents

Contents

Introduction

What of it, if some old hunks of a sea-captain orders me
to get a broom and sweep down the decks? What does
that indignity amount to, weighed, I mean, in the scales of
the New Testament? Who is not a slave? Tell me that.
Well, then however they may thump and punch me about,
I have the satisfaction of knowing that it is all right: that
everybody is one way or other served in much the same
way—either in a physical or metaphysical point of view,
that is; and so the universal thump is passed round.

Herman Melville, *Moby Dick*[1]

In this book we shall examine the way in which the universal
thump of doubt, despair, dying, and all that seems against us can
be used in the spiritual formation of a Christian style of life.

The word "death" has always meant more than physical death.
It represents not only the final limits of life, but also the limitations
against which we work all through our lives. And so the phrase
which is the title of this book, "dying into life," is not meant to
refer to physical death, nor to a way to heaven. In Christian history
it is an image taken from the letters of the apostle Paul, and I
will use it to refer to the tradition which has grown out of his teaching.

Life and death, from a philosophical point of view, are two
aspects of a great mystery. It is not that we have life and then
death, but that death is never absent from life and dying is a
dimension in all our living. "Darkness" might be another image
with which to say the same thing, but "dying" cuts deeper. "I am
in the dark" does not convey the pain and poignancy of "I am
dying." This is because it is *the* image to put up against life. We

[1] (Boston: Spencer Press, 1936), pp. 3-4.

do our living in the presence of dying, and all through life we live and die our way.

Neither is this to say that dying is all evil. The problem is deeper than that. Diamonds would have no value if they were as plentiful as the sand, and life would have no meaning without the limits of death. It can be said that we love our children more because we know that our time with them will come to an end. In this sense, life without the pressure of death would lose much of its character. Taken together then, life and death, living and dying, must somehow be brought together into a style of spiritual formation.

How can we use dying in the service of life? In life there is a reaching out for contact with a larger world. There is growth and vitality. But whereas there are some things we can do, there are other things beyond our control, and at some point we all despair. We work for growth, but life is elusive and we find we cannot lay hold of the deeper realities—love, life, and God. Active reaching, what we might call a "growing into life," is not enough. It takes a deeper experience, first with a reaching out and then with all the patience and emptiness of waiting and receiving. This double movement which leaves us hollow before the coming of God is a "dying into life."

In this book I will maintain that "dying into life" is a historical approach to life and truth which should prove helpful in our secular age. And so I will use the word "dying" to suggest a denial, but not a destruction, of the self. It is doubt and despair. It is suffering and sickness, shame and social ostracism, and all the pressures of life which stand against us. "Life" and "rising," on the other hand, are the opening up and receiving that can grow out of the dying and lead to a positive good. Taken together as "dying into life," this experience is humility, a dying to self and a rising into the life of God. This book is a study in the history of Christian humility.

1 Apostolic Dying into Life

He, of his gentleness,
Thirsting and hungering
Walked in the wilderness;
Soft words of grace he spoke
Unto lost desert-folk
That listened wondering.
He heard the bittern call
From ruined palace-wall
Answered him brotherly;
He held communion
With the she-pelican
Of lonely piety.
Basilisk, cockatrice,
Flocked to his homilies,
With mail of dread device,
With monstrous barbèd stings,
With eager dragon-eyes;
Great bats on leathern wings
And old, blind, broken things
Mean in their miseries.
Then ever with him went
Of all his wanderings
Comrade, with ragged coat.
Gaunt ribs—poor innocent—
Bleeding foot, burning throat,
The guileless young scapegoat:
For forty nights and days
Followed in Jesus' ways,
Sure guard behind him kept,
Tears like a lover wept.
            Robert Graves, "In the Wilderness" [1]

A study of the life of Jesus must come to terms with his suffering and dying as well as with his resurrection rising. In apostolic

[1] Copyright © 1958, 1961 by Robert Graves. Used by permission of Collins-Knowlton-Wing.

Christianity, Paul shaped a style of spiritual formation as a symbolic reliving of the life of his Lord.

The Jewish Basis for Christian Dying

The Jews were a positive people. And the apostle Paul was a Jew, a Pharisee of the Pharisees, and very obviously proud of his heritage. The great positive discovery of ancient Israel was the living God. Yahweh is God of the world, he has revealed himself in the mighty deeds of Hebrew history, and his presence is to be felt everywhere with profound reverence. Here there is no void, no great emptiness beyond creation. In the Jewish style of life there are commandments, and by Paul's day an ethical code had been spelled out in minute detail. The Jews were undoubtedly a very positive people, but beneath their affirmation there were two major ways in which they experienced a great negation.

The first negation was their recognition that God is hidden. Modern man also wrestles with the hiddenness of God, but in Israel this truth was perceived from the opposite direction. Whereas we can feel empty of spirit, the ancient world view was peopled with spirits and local divinities, the hilltop gods of Canaan and the baals in the morning dew. Moses' discovery was not that there is Aliveness in life, but that there is but one God that really matters. And this God, to them as well as to us, was hidden. From the very beginning of Israel's history God was known in a negative way. In Moses this is made clear in two prohibitions. On asking to see God he was told that "man shall not see me and live" (Exod. 33:20). The Ten Commandments demand this same negative approach in their worship: "You shall not make for yourself a graven image" (Exod. 20:4). Through Israel, Paul inherited this sense, not that God was negative, but that he was hidden and could not be seen.

A second way in which Judaism recognized the negative was the way in which the invisible God was made known. To the prophets God was overwhelmingly real, but his presence was known through an experience of self-negation. As a form of knowledge, it was not like touching or seeing; it was not positive in that way. There is a sense in which God must find man, rather than man finding God. And the experience into which God comes is that of "a broken spirit . . . a broken and contrite heart" (Ps. 51:17). This experience of deep humility before God underlay prophetic Judaism, and through it Paul inherited a sense of his nothingness before God.

In these two ways, the hiddenness of God and the nothingness of man, Judaism prepared Paul for the creation of a life style of Christian dying. In our day we also know that God is hidden. For some he is dead. But the secular spirit of the modern world is not broken and contrite, it does not create the openness of prophetic Judaism before the presence of God.

The Development out of Judaism

Paul was a Jew before he was a Christian. In this section we will contrast the change in perspective from the Jewish life style with its negative apprehension to the Christian way with its deliberate dying into life.

The Judaism of Paul's day was largely a religion of attainment, a positive way of growing into life. For a thousand years and more Judaism had been distinguished by its remarkable social character. It began as a national religion, and it never lost its pronounced social consciousness. The inspiration and suffering of the Jewish people found articulate expression in the literature of the Old Testament, and the lessons of its history as a nation were distilled and codified as religious law. In the Torah some 248 positive precepts and 365 negative admonitions provided a fence within which the conscientious Jew must walk. Judaism has always stressed the prevention of sin more than its forgiveness. George F. Moore admits that any religion that sets out to regulate behavior inevitably tends "to imprison the pietists in a somewhat rigid formalism," [2] but this was not Judaism's intention. The good Jew of Paul's day hoped for the life of religious inspiration conveyed through obedience to the Jewish law.

In seeing Judaism as a religion of positive attainment, one must be careful not to exaggerate this direction. The New Testament, for instance, generally condemns the Pharisees as thoroughgoing legalists. There were, of course, strict Jews who equated spiritual

[2] Moore, "The Character of Judaism," *Contemporary Thinking About Paul,* ed. Thomas S. Kepler (Nashville: Abingdon Press, 1950), p. 73.

correctness with the keeping of the law. With them, any slight infraction would spell a total failure of the religious life. Although the first-century records are far from conclusive on this point, it is probable that an exact legalism was never typical of the religion as a whole. There was always a good deal of individual latitude, especially in the field of ideas. There was only one major exception to this. Since the religious life of the nation was held together by ceremony, the authorities felt they had to be more rigid in enforcing ritual orthodoxy. In this area alone would the social character of Judaism approximate a thoroughgoing legalism. "For the most part," as C. G. Montefiore writes, "it taught a gradual process in goodness and knowledge and the love of God." [3]

The kingdom of God is the goal of human history for both the Christians and the Jews, but Christianity shaped a far more negative style of spiritual formation as a way of reaching this goal. The Jewish approach is positive: "Salvation was not a normal Jewish concept. . . . Judaism was and is a religion of attainment." [4] "Conversion was not a normal experience of Judaism." [5] With these descriptions Christian scholars have tried to catch the spirit of the Jewish style. The good Jew hopes to stay within the fence of the law, and so scholars, not prophets, have been their most honored men. It is a reasonable, positive way of life; it does not try too much and it does not fall too far. "Judaism knows," writes Rabbi Joseph Klausner, "that the nature of man will always be human nature and not angel nature." [6] Montefiore recognized how Judaism contrasted with Christianity: "The Rabbinic Jew did not seek to become one with God; he knew, but made little use of the idea of dying to live." [7] The Christian, in hoping for more, must feel that he is less, and here we get a sense of original sin. The extremes, both positive and negative, are heightened and deepened, and the way in which Paul resolved this tension lay in creating a style of Christian dying.

[3] Montefiore, *Judaism and St. Paul* (London: M. Goshen, 1914), p. 50.
[4] Donald W. Riddle and Harold W. Hutson, *New Testament Life and Literature* (Chicago: University of Chicago Press, 1946), p. 97.
[5] Mary H. Andrews, *The Ethics of Paul* (Chapel Hill: University of North Carolina Press, 1934), p. 147.
[6] Klausner, *From Jesus to Paul* (New York: Macmillan, 1944), p. 609.
[7] *Judaism and St. Paul*, p. 85.

The change in perspective might be summarized in this way. The God of the early Christians was still the invisible God of the Old Testament, and in our nothingness before God we are still to recognize our sinfulness. In these ways Christianity continued the insights of prophetic Judaism. But these insights are now set within a negative trajectory: Jesus' call to repentance, Paul's dying into life, and the almost totally negative wrench in John's demand that we be born again. The old negative Jewish apprehension was now transformed so that it could become a central feature in a new style of life.

These differences, of course, must not be pressed too far. We always have so much to learn from Judaism, and most of us in the Western world will always seem to be, like Paul himself, Jewish Christians. Probably the great mass of Christians live out of an essentially positive experience, and all through history individual Jews have crossed a threshold of consciousness to come alive to a dying and rising. But it is important to recognize that a genuine difference does exist. John B. Cobb, Jr., notes that there was an "effective emergence of a new structure of existence . . . [through the] impact of Jesus' transformation of Jewish teaching combined with his resurrection appearances." [8] Paul understood this transformation; he himself was given a new style of life which led him out of the Jewish experience. Montefiore was right in saying that "his psychology is not ours." [9] In teaching "a dying life, not a living death," [10] Paul shaped the classic statement of the new life to which he had been led by the Lord Jesus Christ.

Jesus as "the Lord of Life and Death"

Jesus is the inspiration of the new Christian style of life. Probably no religion is so dominated by its founder as Christianity is by Jesus Christ. This is what makes it puzzling to realize that it was Paul, not Jesus, who worked out the psychology of a style of Christian dying.

[8] Cobb, *The Structure of Christian Existence* (Philadelphia: Westminster Press, 1967), p. 109.

[9] Quoted in T. R. Glover, *Paul of Tarsus* (New York: George H. Doran Co., 1930), p. 77.

[10] William R. Inge, *Christian Mysticism* (New York: Meridian Books, 1956), p. 11: "Mysticism enjoins a dying life, not a living death."

17

Humility is the great theme of Jesus' life, and it can be recognized in all the levels on which he lived. I mean humility in the sense of "something approaching a formal pattern" [11] of humiliation and exaltation. Take, for instance, the teaching of his public ministry. So many of his sayings can be arranged to illustrate a dying and rising experience:

Repent	for the kingdom of God is near.
Blessed are you poor,	for yours is the kingdom of God.
Blessed are you that hunger now,	for you shall be satisfied.
Blessed are you that weep now,	for you shall laugh.
Unless you turn and become children,	you will never enter the kingdom of heaven.[12]

Or consider the emphasis on humility in his parables—the Pharisee and the publican or the rich man and Lazarus. Or reflect on Jesus' own life of humility and all the dying through which he suffered. He knew that his baptism was an initiation into death. In his cry from the cross he knew the void of doubt, despair, and dying. The cross itself, of course, is the chief symbol of negation in his life. It suggests the dual experience, creative as well as corrosive, of this pattern of dying into life. The Christian style of life very plainly found its inspiration in Jesus.

The problem that Paul faced, however, was that we cannot really understand the way in which Jesus lived the life of humility. It was by the grace of God, and we simply do not know how it was possible. In our day scholars have tried to penetrate his personality. Many modern scholars believe that Jesus used none of the titles for himself which Christian history has attributed to him—Son of God, Son of Man, and Messiah. They are all honorific, ages old, and meant to reflect the special position which he has in our hearts. This means that Jesus defines the titles; the titles do not define Jesus. The most we can say of Jesus' self-understanding is that he

---

[11] James M. Robinson, *A New Quest of the Historical Jesus* (London: SCM Press, 1961), p. 121.

[12] *Ibid.* (Matt. 4:17; Luke 6:20-21; Matt. 18:3.)

considered himself the last and unique messenger of God, who was to call men to repentance before the end of the world. But beyond this we cannot go, and the saints have made this surprising discovery in their own experience. Despite their own personal growth in grace, the gap between their experience and Jesus' seems to widen. In this sense he always comes to us as one unknown. And so we turn to Paul, the best interpreter of Jesus, for a psychological understanding of dying into life.

Paul's Own Dying and Rising

The first Christians were a simple people, uneducated and with little sense of sophistication. How could it be otherwise among the peasantry and the urban poor in the first century? It is more than a minor miracle that we had Paul, a man who "gave the religion of Jesus the form in which it was capable of conquering the world without receiving damage to its soul." [13] His experience, though certainly not common in the early church, provided the basic interpretation of dying and rising with Christ.

Paul was born to Jewish parents in the Western Diaspora sometime between 10 B.C. and A.D. 10. "A Hebrew born of Hebrews" (Phil. 3:5), he was beyond question a loyal Jew brought up within the fence of the Jewish law. Luke credits him with an education under the great rabbinical teacher Gamaliel, but most modern scholars believe this unlikely for a number of reasons, and it is never mentioned in Paul's letters. As a Pharisee, however, he would have had religious training and discipline, though not necessarily a highly intellectual education, and his one hundred or so quotations from the Old Testament show him to have been a faithful student of the Jewish Bible. As a Jew of the Diaspora, Paul was also undoubtedly affected by Gentile influences, perhaps especially by the bleak, pessimistic Hellenistic view of eternity. Greek was his mother tongue, but he very seldom quotes Hellenistic authors, and his style of writing shows little classical influence. Arthur Darby Nock summarizes his early life in calling him "externally Hellenic, but inwardly Jewish." [14] This is a conservative statement that probably

---

[13] Gustav Adolf Deissmann, *Paul, A Study in Social and Religious History* (New York: George H. Doran Co., 1937), p. 146.

[14] Nock, *St. Paul* (London: T. Butterworth, 1938), p. 237.

does not do full justice to the Hellenism we will find in his letters. For our purposes we might say that he was born into a religion of attainment.

How can we account for his conversion? What prompted him to create the life style of Christian dying? One clue might be his dedication as a Pharisee. This sect numbered about six thousand in Palestine in the first century. Since their origin at the time of the Maccabbean revolt, the Pharisees had sought to interpret the religious law within the customs of Jewish daily life. By Paul's day they had created a maze of regulations to assist the pious Jew in following the law in every area of activity. If he was one of the strictest, as he claimed, a partial failure in any area spelled total defeat. In this respect Paul's Jewish experience could have been unstable, but we really cannot be sure.

A more likely cause for Paul's conversion experience would have been his self-consciousness and a compulsive perfectionism. As a Jew he was a Pharisee, and as a Christian he was continually dissatisfied with any but an ideal state of things. Both as a Jew and as a Christian he expressed this self-conscious perfectionist drive with the energy and talent of genius. Here I think we are identifying intensity and a high sense of individuality as characteristics that troubled and then blessed all seven of the men we will study in this book. Call it intensity, or classify it as a very advanced stage of personal development, but something in Paul was already dying before Jesus called him back into life.

In his conversion Paul believed that his whole life had been brought to a standstill and then regenerated on a different level. Something died, something came to life, and the process of dying and rising became the normative experience of his life. As a Jew he had persecuted the peasant followers of a new apocalyptic sect. Then, as Luke tells the story, a voice spoke to Paul on the Damascus Road. At first he failed to recognize that it was Jesus. Then he learned that his life was directed against a new revelation of the truth. Still in command of his senses, he reversed his stand as a Pharisee, he called for help from the Christian Ananias, and he asked to serve the cause he had been persecuting. His conversion meant a complete denial of his former position and a willingness to follow the one who met him on the road. This radical reversal of his experience contains a dying and rising characteristic of Christian humility.

His Understanding of the Risen Lord

Paul's experience gave him a way of interpreting Jesus' life, and Jesus' life gave Paul a way of interpreting his experience. That is to say, there was a dying and a rising in both Jesus and Paul. In Jesus it was his actual dying and rising from the dead; in Paul it was the dying and rising within his experience. In this section we will look at the way in which Paul understood the Risen Lord.

A little fragmentary hymn contained in Philippians 2:5-11 gives us a rough outline of Paul's understanding of Jesus which Paul presented elsewhere in his letters. It is a description from the point of view of a Christian who lived in the ancient world, and from our perspective it may appear strangely different.

"Jesus preexisted his life on earth as a heavenly being," to paraphrase Paul; "he came to earth, and he was born as a man. He was obedient unto death on the cross, and so God raised him from the dead to make him the ruler of the universe." The title that was given Jesus is "Lord," a title taken from the Hellenistic world but now very obviously Paul's favorite. To us it may seem to imply simply lordship, but to Paul it suggested not just honor but the ultimate power of creation. It is not a title one would be given at birth, but a title which Jesus won through sharing our existence as a slave. Paul is saying that it is through suffering and death, through dying and rising, that Jesus became the ruler of the universe. He must be seen in his weakness as well as in his strength. He suffered the human situation through which all men must pass. The climax of his life was the cross, and because he was victorious on the cross he was appointed the Lord of creation.

Paul made a truly revolutionary discovery in recognizing that both dying and rising define the character of the Risen Lord. No one else seems to have understood Jesus' full humanity. Peter could not conceive of a suffering Messiah during Jesus' lifetime. Luke never thought of the cross as the saving event. And Matthew, Mark, and John hedged their bet by recognizing the cross but also picturing Jesus as one who is never fully human, one who is always in some sense the divine man. But Paul's Jesus, despite his preexistence as a heavenly being, is still a real man. Here there are no miraculous healing legends to explain away death, no casting out of demons through superhuman powers. Rather, Jesus becomes the Lord through his weakness and not through his strength. Real dying is followed by a very real rising, and on the Damascus Road, Paul believed that he had, not what later Christians were to call a mystical vision, but a resurrection appearance of the Risen Lord. And one day, Paul wrote, the Lord Jesus will give the power which he won over death at his crucifixion back to God. (I Cor. 15:28.) Then God will be all in all.

Paul's understanding of Jesus led him to this conclusion. We are to imitate Christ. "Be imitators of me, as I am of Christ," he wrote to the Corinthians (I Cor. 11:1). Some years ago this and other passages were taken to mean that we should imitate the historical Jesus of the Gospels; that by walking "in his steps" we would help bring in the kingdom of God through a life of love and kindness. Paul meant something quite different. We are to imitate the Lord Jesus Christ in a life of dying and rising with him. We are to imitate not just the goodness and the kindness, but the whole life of the preexistent Redeemer who suffered and triumphed through the full range of human consciousness. Paul said that we are to imitate his example because his apostolic experience of dying and rising is the real way of following the Risen Lord. In our day Albert Schweitzer has said that we must add discipleship to the Ten Commandments; we are to follow Jesus not just in obedience, but in creating a style of life that conforms to his.

The Way in Which Salvation Works in Us

Paul's understanding of our salvation will at first seem just as new and strange as his understanding of Jesus, but in his amazing sense of the significant, he again demonstrates his basically realistic insight into life. Those who accept their own lives as a cross will rise to know a resurrection life in which Jesus Christ is Lord. Here is a description of the way in which Paul understood man's salvation:

We are born, Paul believed, into a world that is now dominated by suffering and death. God created it good, the first Adam was

22

sinless and immortal, but this first man allowed sin to reign, and through him we have inherited a tendency to sin. The world is now under the control of demonic forces. We can capitulate to these forces and take the nature of an animal. (Rom. 1:23.) But in his life Christ overcame the powers of evil and defeated the enemy Death. Through his power we can be restored to our full humanity, and in imitating his life we will find ourselves empowered by his Spirit. All that we are—soul, spirit, flesh, conscience, heart—all that we are is dying and will die. All that we are except our bodies will die. Our flesh will die, but not our bodies—the structure of what we are. Then at death we will put off our earthly bodies and put on a heavenly body so that the continuity of our self will continue in a new life with God.

Paul's description of the Christian life might continue in this way: Our new life in Christ is a fully human life that knows both the cross and the resurrection. We walk in the flesh, but not according to the flesh. We participate in the world but with an inner aloofness, as free men in whom the victory has been won. And we are joined through the church to the body of Christ, that body which is the preexistent Redeemer, the Lord of the cult who is also the Lord of creation. In following him, although we are still dying, we are already entering into eternal life. We are still in the flesh, still responsible for our brother—this has not been stripped from us. But by the grace of God we are being given a new self-understanding through which we no longer belong to this world. We belong to God.

At some points Paul's understanding of man's salvation may seem curious and contradictory. His belief that man's spirit, soul, and flesh may die, but that his body is indestructible, requires an explanation. His opponents, the Gnostics, believed that man is essentially spirit, and that we are saved from the body as our spirits go up into God. But Paul cannot accept this Gnostic idealism which strips off the body with all its individuality and with all the responsibilities of life. We are not saved from this world but in this world, not from suffering but in our suffering, not from the cross but through the cross. For this reason Paul makes the body, rather than the soul or the spirit, the vehicle for carrying on the continuity of human life. He preached not the salvation of the soul, but the resurrection of the body. And so though Paul may seem to

23

give a peculiar definition of body, he does this to protect the whole process of dying and rising with Christ in a real, historical world.

I find Paul's understanding of the resurrection of the body one of his most exciting insights. It is consistent with his emphasis on the psychosomatic unity of man. There is always the Gnostic invitation—to lose our individuality and be absorbed in God. But Paul sensed that we must maintain our integrity both here in this life and in the new form of heavenly existence. John of the Cross, the Renaissance mystic we are to study in Chapter III, looked forward to eating artichokes in eternity. This may have been a poetic rather than a real hunger, but it is Pauline in its emphasis on human wholeness. In Paul we are to accept all the dimensions of man's existence; the joy and happiness, and also the disaster and death. All that we are must be bound together into a single form: "as dying, and behold we live" (II Cor. 6:9). And it must be given direction: "In accepting one's death there is life for others; in suffering, there is glory." [15] And the experience out of which we are to live, and in which we are already being saved, must be understood as a participation in Jesus' suffering and death, and then in the continuing joy of Easter morning.

Strength Through Weakness

Paul's understanding of the Christian life should change our expectation of what is possible in human existence. The saints are not above suffering. Dietrich Bonhoeffer wrote that "it is not some religious act which makes a Christian what he is, but participation in the suffering of God in the life of the world." [16] This includes Jesus: "The summit of saintliness is not in the illusory certainty of being without sin. It is revealed to us, on the contrary, by Christ when he accepts death by assuming all the sins of the world." [17] The Christian life has a surprisingly negative style and positive goal.

An interesting illustration of this is contained in Paul's description of himself in II Corinthians 12:1-10 as the man "caught up to the third heaven." This is his own personal request for healing

[15] Robinson, *A New Quest of the Historical Jesus,* p. 123.
[16] Bonhoeffer, *Prisoner for God* (New York: Macmillan, 1960), p. 166.
[17] Denis de Rougemont, *The Devil's Share* (New York: Meridian Books, 1956), p. 201.

cast in the form of an "aretalogy," a traditional Greek healing story with its very definite structure.[18] Such aretalogies were engraved on stones which were set up in some of the Greek temples. The name of the person was given, the disease was stated ("a dreadful godless fever"), the healing was presented, and the god was thanked with a catalog of how one had been helped. In this passage which was sent to the church at Corinth, Paul created a perfect aretalogy, but he transformed the meaning to make it a confession of how the Lord really came to him and how he comes to us.

The story begins with Paul's description of a vision that he had fourteen years earlier. He then speaks of his illness as "a thorn in the flesh." Three times he asked to be healed, and the word of the Lord that came to him is the theme of this book: "My grace is sufficient for you, for my power is made perfect in weakness." That is the healing. Paul then catalogs all the ways in which God's blessing has come to him. So he boasts, not of the simple triumphs usually named by spiritual healers everywhere, but of the disasters through which he has found strength: "weaknesses, insults, hardships, persecutions, and calamities." He then concludes with an equigram: "For when I am weak, then I am strong."

The point Paul makes is that he was healed, not from his sickness, but with a spiritual healing in his sickness. Christ reaches us not in our strength but in our weakness. His opponents would have denied that anyone who was not healed could have experienced God's grace, but Paul answers that it is precisely when you are weak that you can experience the grace of God. The Christian experience is not some higher level of achievement, something superior to life, but the very dying of life itself into which Christ can come.

The Dying and Rising in the Service of Worship

Paul understood baptism and the Lord's Supper as a dying and rising with the Risen Lord. The positive note in both of these services was well known in Paul's day. He, of course, maintained this emphasis: in baptism "we walk in newness of life" (Rom. 6:4), and in the service of Communion we celebrate "the new

[18] I am indebted to Hans Dieter Betz for this illustration given in a lecture presented at the School of Theology, Claremont, California, November 14, 1968.

covenant" (I Cor. 11:25) of our continuing life with Christ. In this respect we learn nothing new from Paul, but he is original in insisting that in both services we must start with Christian dying.

The consciousness of Christian dying is particularly obvious in the service of baptism. "We are buried therefore with him by baptism into death, so that as Christ was raised from the dead by the glory of the Father, we too might walk in newness of life." (Rom. 6:4.) The believer is entombed in water—that is, immersed for a moment as a symbol of his burial with Christ. His baptism represents the rite through which the believer is initiated into Christ's death and then incorporated into his life. It is the great ecumenical sacrament that should unite all Christians everywhere, and in this service we are empowered to put aside everything that separates us in our natural existence. We are no longer Jews or Greeks, men or women, slaves or freemen. These things have died, they are buried, and together we now form a new humanity "in Christ." The Roman Catholic Church keeps the symbolism of baptism alive through holy water sprinkled upon the believers by the priest and in a cup by the church door where one may be reminded that he has been baptized into Jesus' death.

The Lord's Supper is also a symbol of Christian dying. This service, more than anything else in the Christian life, has taught and maintained the experience of dying into life. In Paul's thought it was a memorial of Jesus' death and resurrection. "As you eat this bread and drink the cup," he wrote to the Corinthians, "you proclaim the Lord's death until he comes" (I Cor. 11:26). Does the Communion service also symbolize our death? Not so explicitly as the service of baptism. The focus is on Christ and not on us. But this, of course, is Paul's major point: we are to imitate Christ. His dying is our dying, his rising is our rising. Like him we are to be "a living sacrifice" (Rom. 12:1), a phrase, I believe, which says much the same thing as Christian dying. Paul's call for seriousness in the celebration of the Lord's Supper suggests the godly sorrow which has come to characterize the Communion service. And when Paul conceives of the Lord's Supper as a messianic banquet on the ultimate Day of the Lord, it symbolizes not only our death but the dying of the world itself before the great gift of eternity.

Thus the two major services of the church must be seen as symbols of dying as well as rising. To these we might add Paul's preaching. He said that his major purpose was to present the dying and rising of the Lord. Sören Kierkegaard makes the point: "The religious address has essentially the task of *uplifting through suffering*." [19] No modern preacher finds this easy, but "it is better to go home from church with misgivings and find the task easier than one had supposed, than to go home filled with bravado and become despondent in the living room." [20]

How to Die

Should we create a style of Christian dying? Is it a conscious process? It may not be with most people; it may be forced upon them by life; but self-denial always has a certain value, even if it is not freely chosen. With the apostle Paul, however, Christian dying was deliberately cultivated as a style of life. Not so much, I should add, for itself. That would be masochism. But chosen for what it leads to. In this section I will conclude our survey of Christian dying by presenting some of the ways in which Paul carried this theme into his own life and into the life of the believer.

An experience of dying with Christ must be cultivated throughout the Christian's entire life. We are to be "always carrying in the body the death of Jesus, so that the life of Jesus may also be manifested in our bodies" (II Cor. 4:10). We are to be united with the Lord in "the fellowship of his suffering" (Phil. 3:10 KJV). Of himself Paul wrote, "I am crucified with Christ." (Gal. 2:20 KJV). But so is every other Christian: "For thy sake we are being killed all the day long" (Rom. 8:36). Some of this emphasis on dying is peculiar to the apostle; Paul apparently believed that he was privileged through his extraordinary apostolic suffering to complete the suffering needed before the age could end. (I Cor. 4:9-13.) But most of Paul's references to suffering and dying are directed to all Christians. There is no other way ahead: "If we have died with Christ, we believe that we shall also live with him" (Rom. 6:8). In imitating the life of Christ, the believer must undergo a lifelong self-denial.

But how are we to do this? How, other than in the church

[19] Kierkegaard, *Concluding Unscientific Postscript* (Princeton: Princeton University Press, 1941), p. 390.
[20] *Ibid.*, p. 416.

services, are we to create a life of Christian dying? Is there some special style of mortification we are to practice? Paul would have answered no. Neither he nor Jesus was an ascetic. The life of self-denial is a life of service.

Paul's charismatic gift within the church was to be a missionary to the Gentiles. In serving God and in serving his fellowmen he was led into a natural experience of Christian humility. Some of his dying was simply the hardship of life on the road, some was the growing persecution throughout the Empire, and some was because of his self-conscious, examining mind where the criticism always outruns the achievement. He suffered—we have the catalog of his persecution at the hands of others and we have a confession of the ways in which he failed himself. But the all-prevailing reason for Christian suffering and dying does not depend upon the circumstances of life, the persecution of others, or the failure within ourselves. The believer suffers because he wants to serve—to serve God and to serve man—and the life of service leads naturally into the self-denial of Christian humility.

Paul developed several ways of understanding Christian dying as a lifelong experience. One way was historical. We are caught up in a great cosmic conflict in our struggle against evil. The Christian is summoned to a relentless and all but eternal battle that will leave him with "fighting without and fear within" (II Cor. 7:5). Only the coming of the Lord will deliver us from the world of history. A second way of describing our dying might be considered psychological. Anders Nygren shows the struggling quality of Paul's faith in a commentary on three successive chapters in Romans:

Chapter 6: We are *free from sin*—yet we must battle against it.

Chapter 7: We are *free from the law*—yet we are not righteous according to its criterion.

Chapter 8: We are *free from death*—yet we long for the redemption of our bodies.[21]

[21] Nygren, *Commentary on Romans* (Philadelphia: Muhlenberg Press, 1949), p. 296.

Here the Christian life is represented as both an achieved fact and a struggling experience. But a third way of understanding his lifelong dying would be to say that Paul never considered suffering and dying a special experience. Where most men, like Job, have regarded suffering as abnormal, for Paul it was simply a normal part of the life of being a Christian. This does not mean that suffering is the only theme, or even the major theme, in the Christian life. And Paul would have agreed with Thomas Kelly's wise observation that "we cannot die on *every* cross, nor are we expected to." [22] But Paul's teaching is clear:

In one way or another we are always dying. We must make our self-denial Christian by undertaking it in Christ's name. And then we can dare the paradox of regarding the cross of Christ as something quite normal and necessary.

Voluntary Humility and Annihilation Humility

I have named Christian humility the virtue which best represents Paul's experience of Christian dying. It is helpful to contrast two other types of humility with his experience of Christian denial. One asks too little, the other asks too much, if dying is to lead into the Christian life.

A "voluntary humility," to give a meaning to a phrase from Colossians 2:18, can be defined as the ordinary expression of self-denial.[23] It is a minimal, or at best a moderate, sacrifice. It is one among many virtues, and it does not bring the whole life into tension. The "volunteer" in humility may be the wealthy patron with a very occasional concern for the poor, but it is more likely to be us with the small sacrifices we make for others. This person is not deeply troubled that he might be wrong. A voluntary humility will not run the full risk of being open (dying) before life.

An "annihilation humility," to coin a phrase, is so severe in its denial that one's individuality and very selfhood may be destroyed. It is a maximum sacrifice and it may call for a complete sacrifice of one's integrity as a person. I am not thinking of the soldier in war,

---

[22] Kelly, *A Testament of Devotion* (New York: Harper, 1941), p. 109.

[23] This is from the King James Version. This reference is not understood, although the intention is obviously to disparage the false humility of an opponent. I am creating my own definition.

or the father risking the danger of fire for his children, but of the person who deliberately destroys himself out of a conviction for a cause. This form of humility is less common, but as persons with a martyr complex or as true believers, we can also choose this form of denial.

Judaism and Islam tend to teach a voluntary humility. Perfectly marvelous in their affirmation of life, these two Middle Eastern religions make a great deal of the positive aspects of personality. Islam, with its call to submission before God, still leaves a man free to be himself, and Judaism creates a strong man that can stand against God. The Eastern religions, by contrast, tend toward annihilation humility. Hinduism would absorb the self in God, and Buddhism would deny and destroy the very existence of the self. Man is to merge with God in a union which annihilates his individuality.

Paul's Christian dying is a tension between these two forms of humility. It is more than voluntary and less than annihilation. His aim is not growth into life, nor dying into death, but a dying into life.

I do not mean to disparage these other great religions, nor to suggest that this is an accurate measure, but to provide a useful way of understanding Christian humility. Kierkegaard illustrates these two extremes in the Christian experience: "Only a man of iron will can become a Christian because only he has a will that can be broken." One extreme is the strength of a strong individuality; the other extreme is the brokenness that only a strong man can endure. Paul was this strong, highly individualized Jew, and as a Christian he never lost the sense of Jewish integrity. But now, as a Christian, he was commanded to do the impossible. The Sermon on the Mount maintains that our motives must be impossibly pure. This is an absolute self-renunciation and yet, unlike Hinduism and Buddhism, it still presupposes our selfhood. We are responsible for doing the impossible. This is the tension of Christian humility, both to maintain our integrity as persons and yet at the same time to deny that we can lead our own lives. In the tension of Christian dying we are to open our lives before God, to maintain our individuality, and to invoke the gift of resurrection rising.

How to Rise

Christian dying—both in Jesus' life and in Paul's experience—led to resurrection rising. The Christian, as Karl Barth wrote, "is always both positive and negative, and he is the first because he is the second." [24] Taken together, the dying and rising in the Christian experience form a genuine paradox, and Paul never separated the cross of Jesus from the resurrection. Far from being contradictory, they form a single pattern of humiliation-exaltation which is the basis of dying into life. In this section we will focus on the goal of the Christian life.

Paul's style of resurrection rising is a dynamically growing historical experience. The simplest observation would be to note that it points to the future: "If we have died with Christ, we believe that we shall also live with him." In the future "the dead in Christ will rise first" (I Thess. 4:16). But Christ, who will be our life then, is also our life now: "I have been crucified with Christ; it is no longer I who live, but Christ who lives in me." And since the Resurrected One lives in us now, we have already begun to experience our own resurrection. This is one of Paul's most amazing insights. We are already experiencing the resurrection, and we are already receiving the gifts of a life in the Spirit.

But then Paul, always the supreme realist, makes a reservation—what scholars call "the eschatological reservation." [25] In one sense we are already rising with Christ, but in another sense the resurrection experience still lies ahead of us. We must wait for the great cosmic catastrophe which will usher in the final resurrection on the Last Day. Until then we live in a "time-between," and our experience moves on two levels. As Rudolf Bultmann writes, "The

[24] Barth, *The Epistle to the Romans* (New York: Oxford University Press, 1933), p. 231.

[25] James M. Robinson presented an understanding of the "eschatological reservation" in a course on "The Pauline School" at the Claremont Graduate School, February through May, 1967. Thus:

Romans: We have died and we will rise.
Colossians: We have died and we have put on Christ, but it is hidden and not yet revealed.
Ephesians: We have died and we have risen, but it is an inheritance in heaven until we acquire possession of it.

In this way Paul's followers keep the eschatological reservation and maintain the tension.

believer must still become what he already is, and he is already what he shall become." [26] We live in this tension. In one sense we have risen with Christ, but in another sense we must still look to the future for the salvation of our bodies. The power of our baptismal resurrection gets us over the top, it lets us endure our present suffering, and it enables us to anticipate a future resurrection which is now made present by faith. In some sense, then, we are rising with Christ.

And what is this resurrection experience like? What is its life? There are really two answers to give. The first answer is Christ: the new life is "in Christ." This phrase seems to have been Paul's own creation. Over half of his references to Christ use the phrase "in Christ." In his letters he never speaks of being one with God or being in God. We can say that fellowship with Christ, not union with God, is the language that Paul uses. This life in Christ, then, is distinctive and sharply defined. It is cultic; that is, the believer is joined to Christ in the fellowship of the church. Yet, as a second answer, we must define the resurrection life in human terms. Christ's truth is the truth of creation, and life in Christ is a genuine human life in the midst of the world. It is not a special life which Christianity has created. The Christian life is the love of God which was always here and which has now come alive for us through dying and rising with the Risen Lord. Nothing anywhere can now separate us from his love. This means that the resurrection life is not something above or apart from the world, but the life of God in the give-and-take of everyday existence.

Love, joy, and peace are characteristic of the resurrection life. So are ecstatic gifts like speaking in tongues. This is because God's power can move through all the levels of human experience: the level of love, the level of intelligence, and the old archaic and subliminal forms of consciousness out of our still living past. Paul created a life style which was tremendously versatile. He could find God's Spirit on all these levels, and for the sake of others he could "become all things to all men" (I Cor. 9:22).

I see him as an energetic, almost driven, little man, always tremendously alert to the immediate situation. Traveler and tentmaker,

[26] Bultmann, *History and Eschatology: The Presence of Eternity* (New York: Harper, 1957), p. 48.

a stern judge of others and a sharp controversialist, the author of the Bible's great chapter on love and a responsible administrator of his churches, and Christianity's greatest thinker. The life of resurrection rising, if Paul can be used as an illustration of his own thought, is a bursting unity of opposites. And when he asks us to imitate him as he imitates Christ. I take this to mean that Paul's life, with all its immediate involvement with dying and rising in historical reality, is the way to go.

The March of the Penitentes

Christian dying was once a very common experience, and people expected the Christian life to include suffering, self-denial, and sacrifice as well as love, joy, and peace. In most churches there were a few forms of mortification which were expected of everyone—tithing, fasting, prayer vigils, and things to give up for Lent. Today most of this is gone. And yet a sense of it remains; humility is often dimly perceived as the way to reality, and perhaps an old tradition of Christian dying can stir us to feel again the need for sacrifice.

When I was a student at the University of New Mexico, I received an invitation to attend the concluding services of Holy Week at the Penitente pueblo of Cordova in the Sangre de Cristo Mountains north of Santa Fe. It was a cold March twenty-third when we arrived toward dusk on Good Friday evening. I was told that we would not have to wait long for our first view of the flagellants, an old penitential order that still observes the literal forms of Christian dying.

Then, to the desolate sound of *pitos* (wood flutes) and the lash of the *disciplinas* (cactus whips), seven *penitentes* came down the road. Circling from the *morada* (the house of the Brotherhood) to the *iglesia* (the parish church), they beat themselves bloody to the bottom of their *pantalones*. Finally as Christ died in the *Tinieblas* service, the candles were extinguished one by one. The crowd came alive with *sudarios* (ceremonial prayers) and wooden clackers to represent the earthquake, and we were out again in the cold midnight air.

I was very much surprised by my reaction. It should have seemed horrible, especially with the knowledge that men used to be crucified, perhaps inadvertently, to a death from exposure as the

Christus. But the penance that night seemed so much a part of my own life. Not that masochism is justifiable. Worse yet would be the criminal tendency to do penance before committing the crime. But we all have doubt and despair, suffering and dying, as part of our lives. We all try to do some kind of penance, not just to atone for the past, but to open the way for the future. I can understand the *penitente* saying: "To those who do not know how to suffer, all life is death."

Christian history is a long penitential procession, and there are many styles of Christian dying. The apostles knew red martyrdom— hardship, suffering, persecution, and death. In its struggle with the Empire the church created a martyr type, a Jehovah's witness that actually hungered for persecution. With the Edict of Toleration in A.D. 313, however, the persecution officially came to an end. Some were thankful that the suffering was over; others risked death as missionaries beyond the frontier; but still others began to realize that dying and rising is part of what it means to be a Christian. They began to choose white martyrdom, a consciously chosen way of dying as preparation for the coming of the Lord. In the early Middle Ages we have the monks with their objective forms for a way of dying into life. For them life was to be a perpetual Lent. In the late Middle Ages we have the mystics with their deeply subjective forms of Christian humility. But by now dying was taking on structure, the tension was going, and it was Luther who rediscovered the apostolic experience of dying in the midst of the world. He knew that he was dying and rising, "totally damned and totally justified," and both at the same time. In our day these expressions of dying may seem foreign at first, but with a little reflection we can understand what they were trying to do. A conscious acceptance and use of suffering must somehow be built into life.

Suffering Is the Path of Consciousness

There are two good reasons why suffering is inevitable: one is the nature of human consciousness, and the other is the nature of God.

With classical Spanish bravado Miguel de Unamuno asserts that "suffering is the path of consciousness. . . . To possess consciousness of oneself is to feel oneself distinct from other beings, and this feeling of distinction is only reached through an act of collison, through the sense of one's own limits." [27] All of us have an awareness of the ultimate insecurity of life, the over-againstness which confronts us as a continual act of collision. There are times when we all know the emptiness of existence. And when we are reflective, we all know that suffering and dying are part of human nature.

There is a great tradition in which God is pictured as suffering. How could it be otherwise if he is love? Judaism also knows a God of suffering and compassion. In his concentration-camp novel André Schwarz-Bart concludes with "Ernie Levy, dead six million times. . . . Yesterday, as I stood in the street trembling in despair, rooted to the spot, a drop of pity fell upon my face." [28] This tender quality represented by the weeping of God is now being expressed in a number of new ways. In the sixties we learned to think of God in more personal terms, and apparently in the seventies we are beginning to recognize God in the fragile sensitivities of nature. God's suffering nature is good reason for the presence of our own suffering, the lifelong suffering which we call dying.

A Recognition of the Truth

This chapter on apostolic dying into life now concludes with an appeal for a recognition of this truth. Humility is the way of dying and rising. Teresa of Avila said that "humility is not a feeling of inferiority but a recognition of the truth."

Know, then, that you are, and always will be, a troubled spirit. "A broken spirit" is the biblical description of what we must know ourselves to be. In the cloistered virtues of the monastery Thomas à Kempis could claim "a good conscience as the testimony of a good man," but in today's open-windowed universe Albert Schweitzer names "a good conscience as the invention of the devil." Pride and selfishness isolate us, self-pity and regret are the slum of the soul, and even the good man, perhaps especially

---

[27] Unamuno, *The Tragic Sense of Life* (New York: Dover Publications, 1921), p. 140.

[28] Schwarz-Bart, *The Last of the Just* (New York: Bantam Books, 1961), p. 422.

the good man, suffers. He is life's delicate child, and so he must be beginning to despair. Know, then, that you are, and always will be, a troubled spirit.

We are each troubled in our own way, and it is important to discover our own style of humility. Most of us practice a voluntary humility, and we do not sacrifice enough. We develop the necessary ego strength to hold our lives together, but then we find it difficult to reverse ourselves with an openness to others and to God. We do not dare risk a dying into life, and so the mystery of God's presence does not break in upon us. Of course, we do need to maintain our integrity, even before God. James Muilenburg used to ask his Old Testament classes if they would lie for God. The answer should be no. The volunteer in humility does not make the mistake of going too far, but in not going far enough he fails to create the tension of dying which can open out into life.

A few souls seem to go too far in their humility, and they destroy not only their pride but themselves as well. Here is an elderly woman who gives so much to charity, some 70 percent of her income, that she needs to be taught to tithe, that is, to reduce her giving to 10 percent so that she can maintain herself as a person. We all know people who should develop their own individuality and learn to value the contribution they can make to others. Denial and dying must not be allowed to destroy us. Perhaps in our day, however, it is easier to be charitable with those whose humility goes too far than with those who do not go far enough.

The style of Christian humility that is right for each one of us is not easy to know. We are too selfish or too selfless, and we may have no sense of the guidelines for the Christian experience. But this is the great achievement of the apostle Paul. His life and work provide the classic interpretation of how we are to imitate Christ in all his dying and rising into life.

Paul's preaching might lead us to move in this direction. We need to begin with a more conscious acceptance of the cross, the suffering and dying which we can accept in Jesus' name. This should affect us deeply. Alfred North Whitehead wrote that his father, an Anglican priest in a rural parish in southern England, could not read the Passion story without weeping. You too are to weep—for a dying Lord, for your own personal failure, for those who so badly need your help.[29] Dying, with its tears, is the boundary line of life where we must all stand and wait for God.

But, as Paul might continue, we can already be rising into the resurrection life with all its charismatic gifts. In Galatians 5:22 we have a catalog of what we might expect: "The fruit of the Spirit is love, joy, peace, patience, kindness, goodness, faithfulness, gentleness, self-control." The service of *love* and the cause of *peace* were never more urgent. In these troubled days *patience* must be basic, and in the creation of the new life style the most helpful gifts might be *gentleness* and *kindness*. But the gifts do not just grow out of a psychological process. Apostolic dying and rising found its power in reliving the life of its Lord.

[29] In the Middle Ages tears were said to be "the currency of the saints." Weeping is one image of Christian dying.

2 ❧ The Outwardness of the Monk

> Lara was not religious. She did not believe in ritual. But sometimes, to be able to bear life, she needed the accompaniment of an inner music. She could not always compose such music for herself. That music was God's word of life, and it was to weep over it that she went to church.
>
> Boris Pasternak, *Doctor Zhivago*[1]

We live in our meanings, and these have been shaped through a long history of spiritual formation. Paul urged others to imitate him in embarking upon an experience like his own, and his dying into life was imitated in a succession of styles. Some were deliberately cultivated and others were the simple, unconscious "accompaniment of an inner music." In this chapter we will explore its outward expression in the life style of the Benedictine monk.

Can We Reshape Life?

How much can we do in shaping the Christian life? How much must be left to God? This may not be a problem in "growing into life." There the focus is on what we can do. But in "dying into life" we are to gather the wood, and God is to send the fire. It takes an especially sensitive style of spiritual formation.

Boris Pasternak wrestled with this problem in *Doctor Zhivago,* and he tried to come to terms with what we cannot do and what we can. He began with an essentially negative approach: he was appalled by the vast experiment of Soviet Russia:

> Reshaping life! People who can say that have never understood a thing about life—they have never felt its breath, its heartbeat—however much they have seen or done. They look on it as a lump of raw material that needs to be pro-

[1] (New York: Pantheon, 1969), p. 49.

38

cessed by them, to be ennobled by their touch. But life is never a material, a substance to be molded.[2]

All those who would create a positive way of life, Communist or Christian, must suffer this criticism. It is no simple matter to re-shape life.

But, Pasternak continues, we can do something. A more subtle and sensitive style of spiritual formation is possible. We can gather wood for the fire; we can create forms into which God may come; Lara could occasionally "compose such music for herself." Dr. Zhivago, the novel's hero, recognized a form of dying which is life-giving:

> "More vividly than ever before he realized that art has two constant, unending concerns: it always meditates on death and thus always creates life. All great, genuine art resembles and continues the Revelation of St. John." [3]

In this second chapter we will explore the spiritual formation of one of the truly great styles of Christian dying, Benedictine monasticism. Catholicism was an attempt to give objective expression to the apostolic spirit, an attempt to order the religious chaos of the Mediterranean world. And it was a great experiment, "a vast Church such as we shall never more see till God returns upon earth, a House of Prayer as spacious as the whole Western world, built with ten centuries of ecstacy." [4] Monasticism was a part of the process. Our question is this: Can Paul's dying into life be reshaped as a definite, visible style of spiritual formation? In the early Middle Ages the Benedictine monks answered yes.

A New Style for the Apostolic Spirit

The apostolic life style scarcely outlasted the first century. But it came as the climax of the long spiritual development of the Mediterranean people, and it taught a form of consciousness to which men would return again and again throughout Christian history. We can trace the development in this way: the mythical

---

[2] *Ibid.,* p. 338. [3] *Ibid.,* pp. 89-90.
[4] Leon Bloy, *La femme pauvre,* as quoted by Emmanuela Polimeni, *Leon Bloy* (London: D. Dobson, 1947), pp. 47-48.

world view of primitive man, the emerging consciousness of civilization, and the rise of rational consciousness with its new freedom for the individual.[5] To this Paul's Christianity added self-transcendence; that is, it could go beyond itself in a dying into life. "In this direction," writes John B. Cobb, Jr., "there is no possibility of further development, only of refinement and increasing understanding of the reality already given." [6] In imitating Christ the apostle Paul had given the Christian faith its final form, but a form which could be expressed in an endless number of different styles.

Paul's experience was not, and is not, easy to understand, and once he had forced the break with Judaism, there was no single cultural pattern to govern the church. Paul's own life was not easy to follow. We can see him as a wandering preacher, proclaiming the message of the coming kingdom, perhaps succeeding in establishing a fellowship of believers, and then moving on to another city. He taught no fixed ethical system; he could be a realist in looking to the immediate situation, or an eschatologist waiting for the end of the age. He was in but not of the world, and throughout his life he maintained this tension. But the world did not come to an end, and the tension of the early Christians was finally lost. By A.D. 150 the church was choosing responsibilities in the world, and it was left to the Gnostic heretics to try to live above the world. Paul's grasp of both realities, his dying and his rising, was not easy to maintain once the apostolic age was over. A new style of Christian dying would have to be worked out by his successors.

The Masochism of the Martyr

Persecution produced a surprisingly little-known life style in the early Christian martyr. At first the hostility to Christianity was haphazard, local, and personal, and Luke and Paul could still maintain their respect for the Roman government. Within a short time, however, the Christians lost their Jewish privileges, and the local persecutions of Nero and Domitian in the first century gave way to the general proscriptions of Decius, Valerian, and Diocletian in the third. As the persecution grew, it became obvious that an answer had to be found, or the church would be destroyed by the state.

[5] Cobb, *The Structure of Christian Existence, passim.* [6] *Ibid.,* p. 144.

The church met the challenge by creating the life style of the martyr, a person who could become a trained participant in a death struggle with the state. Through the sacraments and the services, the inspiration of martyrologies and the promise of immortality, the rewards of paradise and the threat of hell, a life style developed that could carry one through a harrowing experience and actually rejoice in death. The rewards and punishments were made all but visual, and fellow Christians were strategically placed in the courtrooms, jails, and arenas to watch for signs indicating what the martyr's eventual fate would be. An emotion of overpowering character had been created in the martyr.

Not then, nor today, is this style attractive to most Christians. With the Edict of Toleration it was no longer needed. With the fading of the expectation of the end of the world it would have been difficult to maintain. But its essential failing is that it misunderstands the nature of Christian suffering. It is true that suffering is essential to Christianity and that it will persist as long as we live. But suffering is not something for which we are to hope. The martyr type is often fanatically self-righteous when it should be humble. It can wallow in the enjoyment of its suffering as a form of masochism. Sometimes a saint, particularly a Spanish saint, will seem to revel in suffering. John of the Cross welcomed God's presence as "a sweet cautery, a delightful wound." And Teresa of Avila would cry out: "Rest indeed! I need no rest; what I need is crosses." But this is paradox, the tough pride of a conquistador in the Spanish Age of Gold. Dorothy Day is nearer the truth when she said that her Catholic Worker movement is made up of "martyrs, and saints who can live with the martyrs." To enjoy suffering more than the life to which it should lead is to flirt with mental illness. We can take suffering seriously without becoming literal minded. The martyr won a great victory under very difficult circumstances, but another more sensitive style was needed in the growing Catholic Christianity.

The Immense Achievement of Catholicism

Catholicism is the incarnation of the apostolic spirit in the cultural forms of the Mediterranean world. It is the creation of Christendom. A gradual but enormous change was taking place.

Primitive Christianity, with all its local spontaneity, now gave way to the organizing and hardening processes of the church. It was an age of demolition, but it was also an age of enormous creativity. We who live in a modern age of discontinuity should be sympathetic with their struggle for new styles of spiritual formation.

The Roman Empire was like the modern world in its amazing complexity. The Roman Peace had simply united the Mediterranean cultures into a federation in which the old differences continued unchanged. The religious scene was particularly complex. Celtic Druidism, the Greek Pantheon, Jewish monotheism, and desert astralism flourished in their parts of the Empire. Across these local religions spread the Greek philosophical systems: Platonism, Stoicism, Epicureanism, Skepticism, and the new Neo-Platonism. To these were added an increasing number of Greek and Oriental mystery religions. The Greek Eleusinia, the Cappadocian Mên, the Phrygian Great Mother, the Egyptian Isis and Serapis, the Samothracian Cabiri, and the Persian Mithra, all offered a personal intensity lacking in Stoic apathy, Epicurean self-satisfaction, and Skeptic imperturbability. Among all of these religious and philosophical aspirations there were the no less serious black arts of magic, necromancy, fatalism, animism, and superstitions of every kind. Officially Roman emperor-worship surmounted everything, but in actuality, as in the complex religious scene of Hindu India or modern America, the individual had to provide his own hierarchy of values and "do his own thing."

The church of the early Middle Ages set itself to ordering this religious complexity. The liturgy, for instance, developed a symbolic initiation into the dying and rising of the Christian life. A third century work describes the offices of baptism, instruction, and confirmation as a single successive ceremony.[7] It began with a lengthy all-night vigil, a triple renunciation of Satan, a profession of belief, baptism as the death and burial of the old man clothed anew before the bishop, the laying on of hands for the gift of the Spirit, the anointing and sealing with the sign of the cross, the giving of the kiss of peace, and finally fellowship in the service of Holy Communion. Each step confirmed the new Christian in

[7] Hippolytus of Rome, *The Apostolic Tradition*, as quoted by Massey Hamilton Shepherd, Jr., *The Oxford American Prayer Book Commentary* (New York: Oxford University Press, 1959), p. 271.

his spiritual formation. Greek mysteries were being turned into Roman sacraments. Similarly, new thought and experience, as well as the pressure of heresy, forced the church to define its doctrine. The forms for the new Catholic age proceeded along these five lines—sacramental, otherworldly, ascetic, mystical, and institutional. To the extraordinarily visual-minded people of the Middle Ages, the attempt would be to try and objectify the whole Catholic style of spiritual formation as the City of God made visible on earth.

The monk was the finest expression of the style of life emerging in the early Middle Ages. In the *Divine Comedy,* Dante placed the monks in the highest circle of the planetary heavens, and he set Benedict apart as their loftiest representative.

The Rise of Monasticism

Monasticism[8] began with the official triumph of Christianity, and its greatest achievement was to establish humility as the cardinal Christian virtue. With the more aggressive individuality of the modern world, many Christians are becoming activists, and for them love, often an intolerant love without humility, takes priority. But the medieval monks worked out a pattern of psychological dying that was unchallenged for a thousand years.

Little basis for monasticism can be found in the New Testament. Jesus taught his followers to fast, give alms, and pray, but most primitive Christian asceticism was spontaneous and unorganized. It stemmed from the apostolic disdain for a corrupt and dying world. The triumph of the church did little to soften this pessimism, and the protest that was once directed against the world was now against the increasing power and corruption of the church itself. Beneath these reasons for asceticism—a dying world and the power of the church—there was the deeper reason that is always there.

The old pattern of humiliation-exaltation of the apostolic age was still alive in the Christian experience. It was ascetical in its denial and mystical in its expectation. It soon became apparent that this spirit could be shaped and formed in the life of community. In secluded places where a community could create a controlled

---

[8] Technically, "monachism" is the proper term to use in reference to both monks and hermits. "Monasticism" just refers to monks.

environment, a family of monks could begin to set up a "school in the Lord's service." Together as a community they could re-work the symbolic dying and rising of apostolic Christianity and shape a new style that was peculiarly visible.

The first hermits appeared in the East. Individuals left society for the wilderness. Cenon, a Cilian hermit, ate only one meal a week for thirty years. Sleep, like food, was an enemy to fight, and Pachomius is said not to have slept lying down for the last fifteen years of his life. Hermits and monks and even Jerome so fought bathing that the church killed the public bath. The Boskoi hermits lived by grazing on grass, Simeon Stylites lived on a pillar, and Anthony of the Desert wrestled with the devil. The styles are strange indeed in the great periods of change. Helen Waddell has shown that many of these stories, though probably authentic, are not representative of the whole movement of monasticism.[9] Most of the early monks were hermits who led simple lives of self-denial, but their first ideals were chaotically individualistic.

Monasticism, like the church itself, next turned toward social organization, and the first monasteries appeared in the East. Around the year 300, Anthony and his fellow hermits were spending their solitary lives engaged in making baskets, but on Saturdays and Sundays they came together for worship. At about this time Pacho-mius made a major advance in creating the first cooperative monas-tery. The monks still lived in cells and ate alone, but they shared the common community work and met for services four times a day. Pachomius believed that "to save souls you must bring them to-gether."[10]

The next great step in monasticism was taken by Basil toward the end of the fourth century. He wrote a series of devotional cathechisms which were gradually put into practice throughout the East. All the monks were made to live under one roof, the monasteries were located in centers of need, and everyone was set to work on social concerns such as the care of the poor and or-phaned. In future centuries Basil's emphasis on physical work was given up, and a life of continual countemplation took its place.

[9] Waddell, *The Desert Fathers* (Ann Arbor: University of Michigan Press, 1957).

[10] Herbert B. Workman, *The Evolution of the Monastic Ideal* (Boston: Beacon Press, 1962), p. 88.

Without intellectual and social outlets Eastern monasticism degenerated into sterility. It could produce an occasional Father Zossima in *Brothers Karamazov,* but Dostoevski as well as Tolstoi knew that the startsy, the spiritual directors of Old Russia, were out of touch with historical reality.

Monasticism found no such easy root in the West, but once rooted it developed a balance that could produce great and lasting results. Athanasius is reputed to have introduced monasticism from the East in his visit to Rome in A.D. 339. Martin of Tours served the movement as a practical hero in the founding of a number of communities in Gaul. Jerome, the translator of the Vulgate Bible, lent it his great personal authority. And yet its growth was slow and somewhat amorphous. A new style of spiritual formation was needed to create a monastic ideal in the West.

Roman Character Infused with the Christian Spirit

Benedict was born in about the year 480, in the small Sabine market town of Nursia in the mountains of central Italy. Little is known of his family background, but he seems to have been of good, if not noble, blood. This enabled his parents to send him to Rome for the kind of education common to the privileged classes of that day. His education, however, was soon cut short, and while still in his teens, "skillfully ignorant and wisely unlearned," [11] he left the luxury and corruption that generally attend city life to become a hermit in the Apennines.

We do not know how successful Benedict was as a hermit, but he was not allowed to continue a simple life of seclusion. Country folk discovered his cave and began coming to him for the help he could give. His reputation spread as a wonder worker, and he was forced to organize his followers into a monastic community. The undisciplined monks of his first monastery tried to poison him, and in his second attempt a jealous priest disrupted the community with the dancing of naked prostitutes in the monastery garden. For his third attempt he traveled with a few monks to the beautiful elevation of Monte Cassino, and there in about the year 526 he founded the monastery that was to be his home and the model for Western

[11] Gregory, *The Dialogues of Saint Gregory,* 11, Prolegomena.

monasticism. For fifteen years he ruled an increasing establishment, and out of this experinece toward the end of his life he wrote the *Rule*,[12] a small manual of 108 pages that became the standard discipline for the monastic style of life in the West.

Benedict was a Roman of the Romans, and his style of life can be seen as the Roman character infused with the Christian spirit. The simple farmer-soldier ideal that had made Rome great continued to exist in the Italian countryside. The key to its greatness lay in "the sense of self-subordination which marked the Roman mind. . . . Throughout their history the Romans were acutely aware that there is 'power' outside man, individually or collectively, of which man must take account." [13] This sense of respect before the will of the gods was *pietas;* before the maintenance of freedom, *libertas;* before human relationships, *humanitas;* before tradition, *mores;* before authority, *auctoritas;* before the pledged word, *fides.* An integrated character was to be achieved through discipline. Its achievement would reflect "a responsible cast of mind" in *gravitas,* and it would oppose irresponsibility in any form of *levitas.* Within the cast of mind of the Roman character, there was a peculiar vacuum which the Christian spirit was suited to fill. "Of emotional appeal, of spiritual strengthening, of explanation of life and its immediate problems, Roman religion had little to offer." [14] Its farmer-soldier Stoicism left its followers hungry. Benedict's appeal lay in the way in which his very Roman character was invested with the Christian spirit.

Benedict created a style that admirably suited early Catholic Christianity. A simple, direct way of life was needed that could spell out the Spirit for an illiterate peasantry and still maintain the dying-rising tension of apostolic Christianity. In the time of trouble that was the early Middle Ages, the style would have to be tough and disciplined. Work and obedience would be cardinal virtues; and, both as a Roman and a Christian, Benedict spoke and wrote with a tone of command. When a monk held back a last bottle of oil from a penitent seeking alms, he ordered the bottle

[12] Benedict, *Rule for Monasteries* (Collegeville, Minn.: St. John's Abbey Press, 1948).

[13] R. H. Barrow, *The Romans* (London: Penguin Books, 1949), pp. 218-19.

[14] *Ibid.*, p. 144.

thrown out of a window overlooking a cliff. Authority and discipline, but for the sake of the poor! The style would be rooted in the countryside, even to the point where Benedict, like Francis, is said to have worked miracles with animals. To this day a pet crow is kept at Monte Cassino in honor of the one that prevented Benedict from eating poisoned bread. And above all, the rule must be moderate if it was to appeal to the Western mind. Greek monasticism could go intellectual, mystical, and otherworldly, but the Roman, to reverse Sinclair Lewis' statement, was the ancient American.[15]

In all these ways Benedict represented the objective, visible style of spiritual formation which was attractive to the medieval mind. It is said that whereas others have fought their way *to* God, Benedict fought *for* God. The question is whether his reinterpretation of Christianity destroyed or strengthened the dying and rising experience of Christian humility.

A School in the Lord's Service

In the Middle Ages it was commonly believed that the Christian life called for three conversions:
1. A turning from the world.
2. The training for a Christian life.
3. Attaining direct contemplation of God.[16]

Benedict assumed that every serious-minded Christian had already undertaken the first conversion. The third involved a mystical development that lay beyond the power of monastic regulation. Mystics like John of the Cross devoted their lives to an elaboration of the inner processes of this "union with God." The *Rule* is concerned with this second form of conversion, the form of denial which is a training for a Christian life. Evangelical American Protestantism has often conceived of conversion as a sudden crisis experience to be called forth in a preaching service. In the Benedictine monastery, however, conversion was generally understood to be the training in the Christian life which took place in the monastery as a lifelong experience.

[15] Sinclair Lewis: "The American is the modern Roman."
[16] Ildephonsus Herwegen, *St. Benedict* (London: Sands and Co., 1924), p. 110.

In coming to Monte Cassino, an applicant would wait at the monastery gate for four or five days before he would be recognized and admitted by Benedict. He would then share the monastic life for perhaps a year. If the period of trial proved mutually satisfactory, he would take three vows, first orally and then in the form of a written contract which he placed on the altar. He would promise stability, the conversion of manners, and obedience. These vows strike one as surprisingly unlike the traditional monastic vows of chastity, poverty, and obedience.

The vow of stability meant that a monk promised to bind himself permanently to a particular monastery. He might move with a group of fellow monks to establish a new monastery, or he might be elevated in the church's service, but the vow generally settled the average monk in a specific monastic family for the rest of his life. In the second vow, "the conversion of manners," he committed himself to the monastic life laid down in the *Rule*. And in the third he pledged his obedience to the abbot of the monastery. The vow of chastity was not mentioned because it had long been assumed throughout monasticism. The vow of poverty was also assumed, but here Benedict took pains to define what he meant by poverty. No one was "to have anything of his own, anything whatever." [17] But he could have the use of what he needed, and the Benedictine life was not severe by the standards of the day. And so with "cowl, tunic, stockings, shoes, girdle, knife, pen, needle, handkerchief, tablets" [18] the new monk was equipped for the monastic life.

The monastic life was a balance of three major activities—work, study, and prayer. First, almost six hours were spent each day in some form of work. It took the longest part of the monk's day. The *Rule* calls for "manual labor," [19] but from the beginning the monks worked as craftsmen more than as laborers, and in time the work shifted toward the painstaking handiwork of the copyist. Secondly, an average of three and one half hours a day was set aside for reading. At the beginning of Lent the monks "shall each receive a book from the library, which they shall read straight through from the beginning." [20] This suggests that the monks were basically not a scholarly type. The books were biblical and devo-

[17] *Rule,* ch. 33, p. 49.   [18] *Rule,* ch. 55, p. 71.   [19] *Rule,* ch. 48, p. 63.
[20] *Rule,* ch. 48, p. 64.

tional. Third, the various forms of prayer—the community services and the private meditation—took four and one half hours a day. The religious services were the crown of the Benedictine life. Benedict established that "as a school of God's service . . . the primary community service shall be the celebration of the divine office." [21] In these three ways, then, the monk spent his life. Prayer was the great glory of the monastic style.

Prayer has traditionally been divided into three general types: habitual, private, and public. In the Benedictine monastery all three were practiced, but the main emphasis was on public prayer. In habitual prayer Benedict believed one ought "to devote oneself frequently to prayer. . . . Our prayer ought to be short and pure, unless it happens to be prolonged by an inspiration of divine grace." [22] The apostle Paul wrote of "praying without ceasing" (I Thess. 5:17 KJV), but according to Joachim Jeremias this meant that he prayed according to the frequency of his Jewish heritage, apparently three times a day.[23] The hermits, however, had a goal of continual prayer, and it was against them that Benedict was reacting. Prayer, he believed, should be "frequent," but not "habitual." [24] As to private prayer the *Rule* has little to say. Abbot Butler believes that the early Benedictines may have devoted one and a half hours a day to private meditation.[25] Here, we must remember, Benedict lived before the elaboration of private prayer by the mystics of the late Middle Ages. The great development of extemporaneous prayer was the creation of the Carmelite mystics of the sixteenth century. Public prayer was the major Benedictine emphasis, marking the swing from the hermit's lonely existence to the life of community.

"The Work of God," the daily liturgical services of the monastery, spaced eight formal services throughout the day. In an early Benedictine monastery the daily schedule would look something like this on a typical day late in March:[26]

[21] E. Cuthbert Butler, *Benedictine Monachism* (London: Longmans, Green, 1919), p. 31.

[22] *Rule,* ch. 20, p. 39.

[23] Joachim Jeremias said this in a guest lecture at the School of Theology at Claremont, in California.

[24] *Rule,* ch. 4, p. 16.   [25] Butler, *Benedictine Monachism,* pp. 60-61.

[26] *Ibid.,* pp. 281-82. The day chosen is March 24, just after Easter.

Rise	2:30–3:00
Vigils (Matins)	3:00–4:15
Lauds	4:15–4:45
Meditation	4:45–6:00
Prime	6:00–6:20
Work	6:20–10:00
Tierce	10:00–10:15
Reading	10:15–11:30
Sext	11:30–11:45
Dinner	11:45–12:10
Siesta	12:10–1:30
Nones	1:30–1:45
Work	1:45–5:00
Vespers	5:00–5:30
Supper	5:30–6:00
Collations and Compline	6:00–6:30

The day would extend from the chanting of the fourteen psalms and three lessons in the service of Vigils until the prayers of Compline and "the reading of Cassian's Collations or such book." [27] Then the Great Silence would fall, and the monks would proceed out of the chapel. When it was still dark, long before dawn, the cry *"Benedicamus Domine"* would break the silence, and the monks would rise for worship. A new day.

Throughout Western history a number of fascinating styles of spiritual formation have been achieved within a controlled environment. The Jewish Hasidim, Plymouth Colony, the Amana Community, the·Mormon settlements, and now the hippie commune. Probably none has been more thorough than the Benedictine school in the Lord's service, and certainly none has been more central or made a greater contribution to the Western culture.

The Benedictine Expression of Christian Humility

Humility was the Benedictine expression of Paul's dying and rising with Christ. In the thirteenth century Thomas Aquinas thought of humility as a "subdivision of a subdivision of the

[27] *Ibid.,* p. 280.

50

virtue of temperance." [28] But with Benedict it is not a single virtue like others, but the essence of the Christian life. The longest chapter in the *Rule* is "On Humility," and in it Benedict describes twelve stages of humility through which the soul ascends to the contemplation of God. The stages are not successive, but the first four can be seen as a progressive dying into life.

The monk is to begin with a fear of God that is typically biblical. With Benedict it is a straightforward attitude, not a mystical feeling. Various techniques are suggested to help the monk incorporate this knowledge into his experience. "Let his thought constantly recur to . . . hellfire," or "let a man consider that God is always looking at him from heaven." [29] The ascent toward the transformed life begins with the fear of God. Taken in context, however, it might be characterized chiefly as awe.

"The second degree of humility is that a person love not his own will." [30] This is the submission of the will. A person is not to love his will or take pleasure in satisfying his own desires. He is to model his life on Jesus' example of humility. But note. The submission of the will does not mean self-mortification. In the eleventh century Peter Damiani introduced systematic flagellation into Western Europe. His heirs might be the *penitentes* of New Mexico. But at this point Benedict differs from both his predecessors (the hermits) and his successors in calling for self-surrender rather than self-conquest.

In the third degree of humility the monk is to be obedient to his Superior.[31] The abbot was believed to represent Christ, and his authority was far-reaching and final. The monk's obedience was to be instantaneous. Later on, this meant that a monk should rise from the work of copying without finishing the stroke of his pen. If the abbot is obeyed but "with an ill will and murmurs," [32] the monk will be punished until amends are made. But it is to be the authority of the Roman *pater familias,* strict but reasonable. The abbot is warned not to set up a tyranny, but to provide a watchful care over his family of monks. His aim is the conversion of manners, not the destruction of a man's individuality. Unlike

[28] Justin McCann, *Saint Benedict* (New York: Sheed and Ward, 1937), p. 186.
[29] *Rule,* ch. 7, pp. 21-22.   [30] *Rule,* ch. 7, p. 24.
[31] *Ibid.*   [32] *Rule,* ch. 5, p. 19.

Jesuit obedience, Benedictine does not have the power of compelling a monk to live outside the conditions of the life he has chosen. "We obey a man, but within the limits of our vows." [33] Benedict wanted spiritual, not legal, obedience. Ideally, both the abbot and the monk are to be inwardly obedient to God.

The first three stages of humility (awe, submission, and obedience) culminate in "patience in trial." [34] In the fourth state the dimension of time is added, and patience is to transform obedience into endurance. In medieval Christianity the prolongation of self-denial was called a "white," or bloodless, martyrdom. It contrasted with the "red martyrdom" of the apostles. Benedict's "patience in trial," or, as Abbot Delatte translates it, "heroic obedience," [35] is meant to make the experience of humility lifelong.

The great enemy of monastic humility was acedia, "a kind of dull weariness born of intolerable monotony and the triviality of daily life." [36] It was "the midday demon" (Ps. 91:6) that could eat out a monk's spirit and take possession of his unhappy soul. No threat is more subversive of the religious life in a controlled environment. Like Anteas in the Greek legend, the monk slowly strangles to death above the strength-giving earth. Here is the monk who, though living up to the letter of the *Rule*, "did so blow for weariness of spirit that all would hear him." [37] Against this enemy the monk must rewin his strength within the monastic regimen. He must fight the continuing battle of life with patient obedience. He must work the system—physical labor, study, and prayer—and hold to patience "with a silent mind." The crown of life for red martyrdom was the gift of paradise, but the crown of Benedict's white martyrdom was to be God's peace here on earth.

Pauline Christianity and the Benedictine Spirit

Is Benedict an authentic successor of the apostle Paul? His images are different, and he lived in a different period of history.

[33] Paul Delatte, *The Rule of St. Benedict* (London: Burns, Oates, and Washbourne, 1921), p. 4.

[34] *Rule,* ch. 7, p. 24.　[35] Delatte, *The Rule of St. Benedict,* p. 115.

[36] James O. Hannay, *The Spirit and Origin of Christian Monasticism* (London: Methuen, 1903), p. 154.

[37] G. G. Coulton, *Five Centuries of Religion* (New York: Cambridge University Press, 1923), I, 85.

But is there a sense in which Benedictine monasticism continued the essential experience of apostolic Christianity? That is, is Benedictine humility a way of expressing Paul's dying and rising with Christ? I will use our two contrasting forms of humility, "voluntary" and "annihilation," to present the basic Christian experience which was shared by both Paul and Benedict.

Is Benedictine humility "voluntary"? Is it a minimal or moderate form of self-denial? The *Rule* is unquestionably severe in its teaching. In the chapter on humility three points describe the life style to be achieved through Christian dying—nothingness before God, nothingness before men, and the avoidance of singularity. Taken together they level a devastating attack on every form of pretense. Benedict could hardly have undertaken a more complete annihilation of pride. The monk is to speak as little as possible, he is to hate jests and idle words with Roman vigor, he should hold his head with his eyes toward the ground, and he must "keep death daily before one's eyes." [38] Monastic humility was not a simple voluntary act, but a serious and severe form of psychological dying.

Is Benedictine humility an "annihilation" of human individuality? Does Benedict break the will of his monks? The answer is no if one can appreciate the hard peasant culture in which he lived. Benedictine denial must be considered moderate by the standards of the sixth century. First, Benedict discarded the major characteristics of the far more severe hermit style of life—bodily austerity, individual spirituality, and prolonged and almost continual prayer. Second, the Benedictine life compared favorably with the life style of the Italian peasant of that day. The monks ate two meals a day, just like the farmers, and the monastery refectory offered a choice of two dishes for the main course. Their beds were good, and although they slept together in a dormitory, so did the large Italian family. In the thirteenth century the early Franciscans were to wear clothes so poor that a traveler would not pick them up off the highway, but the early Benedictines dressed in the undyed gray woolens of the Italian peasants. The Benedictine style was the poverty of a carpenter's household in Nazareth, not the poverty of Calvary. And sleep, surprisingly

[38] *Rule*, ch. 4, p. 16.

53

enough, if you will count the siesta, was Mediterranean style, not all at night, and yet still approximately eight to nine hours a day. The moderation is surprising. This is not annihilation humility.

Does the spirit of Benedictine humility crowd a man's sense of integrity? Can a man sustain his own private personal life under the very real pressure of the *Rule?* Benedict's teaching on silence is a good example. It shows that Benedict created a severe style and yet also a few little ways of escape. Here is the general direction: "The ninth degree of humility is that a monk restrain his tongue and keep silence, not speaking until he is questioned." [39] The monk was to cultivate a "silent mind" and to speak sparingly. The Latin word used is *taciturnitas,* not *silentium.* In the seventeenth century Abbot de Rancé founded the Trappist order with an almost perpetual silence, but their "mutism" is not Benedict's sparingness of speech. It would perhaps be easier. The Benedictine monk was to speak little, he would ask permission to speak, and there were a few times each day when he could speak freely. In the *Rule* there are little touches to show that the monks were to encourage each other to rise for Vigils or to correct each other in minor faults. There was pressure, there was undoubtedly great denial, but there were ways in which a monk could preserve himself from annihilation.

The problem again is one of making adequate allowances for life in a peasant society. Sparingness of speech would be very trying and limiting in our garrulous and nervously excitable modern culture. The simple stoic peasants who joined Monte Cassino would not have found it nearly so difficult.

Benedict was continually careful to preserve the individuality of his monks, and the *Rule* has a plaintively personal concern. The monks are not to be considered late for Vigils if they arrive before the "Glory be to the Father" of Psalm 94, "which for this reason we wish to be said slowly and protractedly." [40] On rising they are to "gently encourage one another, so that the drowsy may have no excuse." [41] The monastic families often seem to reflect the sentimentality of a large Victorian family or of a small private boarding school. This was possible because even the great Benedictine houses seldom had more than fifty to seventy

[39] *Rule,* ch. 7, p. 27.   [40] *Rule,* ch. 43, p. 58.   [41] *Rule,* ch. 22, p. 41.

monks. A single death would send the entire family into mourning. According to a later tradition the monk's place at the table would be set in his honor for a full month after his death. There were many little signs of personal consideration.

Kindness was valued highly in the Benedictine monastery. Old men and children were to be treated with "special kindness." And a critical spirit was to be avoided at all times: "When you criticize your brother out of love, suspect that love." This kindly and uncritical spirit, however, must not be allowed to blunt the rigorous Promethean thrust of the individual monk. However considerate he was to be of others, he was still to be hard on himself in maintaining the tension of the monastic life.

A Premature Peace

We are now ready to appraise the style of life in Benedictine monasticism. The Benedictine motto is the single word "Peace," and the aim of the monastery is to be the City of God made visible on earth as the way of peace. It is not the apostolic peace that passes understanding, nor the martyr's peace in paradise, nor the hermit's peace in the conquest of himself, nor the mystic's peace with its ascent into contemplation. It is the peace of a silent mind and simple, heroic obedience. It was a beautiful achievement. The question is whether the Benedictine peace was premature.

The Benedictine life style was a synthesis of the three great movements of its day—the Roman character, the Christian spirit, and the medieval movement toward materialization. Apostolic Christianity with all its freedom and spontaneity had been transformed into the highly objective monastic style of life. In the last paragraph of the chapter on humility Benedict hoped that his monks would be able to live up to the best in the Christian life "by reason of . . . love" rather than fear. And at the end of the *Rule* he hoped again that his monks would be able to rise above "this minimum rule . . . for beginners," but there is nothing to indicate that they would then leave the monastery. Out of his knowledge of the needs of human nature he created a Roman materialization of the Christian ideal.

We can recognize this Roman contribution in the shaping of the monastic ideal. Roman and Stoic theorists had taught that laws are universal and given by the gods. They needed only to be discovered. By Benedict's day, Christianity had accepted the legal theories of the Empire. The church believed that God's law was universal, and that it regulated a host of lesser but still absolute codes. The laws for merchants or for Jews or for the Frankish kingdom were all codes under God's law. John Chapman believes that Benedict was probably commissioned by the pope to write a monastic law for the church.[42] The Roman heritage made this contribution to the materialization of the Christian ideal.

Was the new monastic ideal a continuation of the apostolic experience? In some respects, of course, there was a radical break. According to Pope Gregory, Benedict recognized that the monastic life differed from the apostolic. When he was asked to bring a dead boy back to life, he refused at first on the grounds that this was work only an apostle could do. The medieval Christians believed that they had entered the sixth and last age of history, and that the Christian spirit now required an essentially different kind of life.

One essential difference, as argued by Augustine, was that once the Christian experience had been established, a man's will was sanctified, and in some sense he stood above the dying tension that had produced his conversion. To be sure, the convert was still plagued with imperfections, but these were incidental or "venial" sins and not basic or "mortal." Augustine's Christian was not perfect, but he had begun to rise above the dying tension of Christian humility. His writings illustrate this: "Let us, as many as are running perfectly, be thus resolved that, being not yet perfected, we pursue our course to perfection along the way which we have thus far run perfectly."[43] A kind of perfection has been achieved, and something of the tension of apostolic Christianity had been lost.

This difference between the Catholic and apostolic experience made it possible to create the monastic style of life. John Cassian, the man to whom Benedict was most particularly indebted in his chapter on humility, was condemned by the church as a Semi-Pelagian. That is, he overemphasized what we can do, and not

[42] John Chapman, *Saint Benedict and the Sixth Century* (London: Longmans, Green, 1929), pp. 203-4.
[43] Augustine, *On Man's Perfection in Righteousness*, ch. 19.

what God does, for our salvation. Benedict himself is generally thought of as completely orthodox in his Catholic faith, but there are little touches throughout the *Rule* showing its Semi-Pelagian character. The chapter on humility, for example, closes with the belief that a monk can achieve a state of perfection: "The Lord will deign to show forth by the Holy Spirit in His servant now cleansed from vice and sin." [44] In this Benedict is apostolic in seeking perfection, but Catholic in believing he could achieve it within the forms of the monastic life.

The Benedictine experience was characterized by a simplicity of spirit. The problem, from our point of view, is that this simplicity was tied to a particular expression of the Christian spirit. The *Rule* is a series of regulations for governing the monastic life, and although Benedict believed in this spirit, he also believed in its materialization in monasticism. To be generous, we might say that no conflict needed to exist between the spiritual and the legal in the reshaping of the apostolic spirit. I am impressed with the simplicity of spirit which I find in the *Rule* and which I experienced in my own stay in a Benedictine monastery. But I am just as sure that something in apostolic Christianity has been lost. Something of the "eschatological reservation" is gone. The tension is different. In the first Christian age Jesus was the one materialization of the Spirit, there was no highly stylized way to walk. "For here we have no lasting city, but we seek the city which is to come." (Heb. 13:14.) Now, in the early Middle Ages, there is the tendency to create a new Judaism within Christendom, and a new form of voluntary humility within the Christian experience. The forms of Christian dying are there, but something in the dying is no longer conceived of as a lifelong experience. The peculiar Benedictine heresy/glory is to have won a premature peace.

But times change, no form is final, and the poetic simplicity of the Benedictine peace could not last. The Catholic ideal of the early Middle Ages was destroyed through the enormous elaboration of its own development. The Cistercians chose agriculture, the Cluniacs scholarship, the Franciscans service, the Dominicans preaching, the Jesuits obedience, the Carmelites mysticism, and the Trappists silence. There is no safeguard for simplicity. In time

[44] *Rule,* ch. 7, p. 28.

57

the Benedictine peace stood only as a reminder of another age and a different spirit.

With this growth, moreover, the basic Catholic assumptions were also challenged. The early Middle Ages had Augustine, but the period generally proved unable to develop a high sense of individuality. The Benedictine monks have not been noted for their originality. There is no distinctive Benedictine theology, architecture, mysticism, or method of prayer: "in short, no Benedictine particularism." [45] It took the Renaissance to create the new individuality. It took the Reformation to rediscover the reality of spiritual sins: "the pride of a bishop, the pretensions of a theologian, the spiritual arrogance of the church itself." [46] The Benedictine ideal simply collapsed as a viable life style. When the monasteries began to spread again in the revival of the nineteenth century, they could not return to the simplicity of the early Catholic age. The modern monk no longer fully believes in the materialization of the Spirit; no monk now claims to see demons. Our ten thousand Benedictine monks cannot successfully offer their life style in a secular society.

Three Lessons to Learn

I am attracted by the formal simplicity and the ordered peace of the Benedictine style of life, and I hope that it is possible for us today to transpose three things which they teach into a modern style of spiritual formation.

1. The Benedictine style is incarnational and institutional. In apostolic Christianity, Jesus himself was so immediately present that everything else was tentative. The Jewish cult was abolished. There was no holy place, no sacred time, no temple, and priesthood belonged to Christ. But when men no longer lived out of these messianic hopes, the church needed new forms of immediacy. The Spirit needed to be made flesh in a continuing community. The Benedictine monastery is part of this trajectory as it moves through history. Christianity is simply not possible without many forms of incarnation. That's the whole point. God is involved,

[45] Butler, *Benedictine Monachism*, p. 306.
[46] Reinhold Niebuhr, *The Nature and Destiny of Man* (New York: Scribner's, 1943), I, 59.

as Kazantzakis writes, in an "erotic march through flesh." [47] In an age of institutions the incarnation must become institutional. We need to commit ourselves to this, and for most of us this will now take a series of individual decisions. No commune will command all our allegiance, and each of us will choose to belong to a series of communities—family, local, academic, vocational, scientific, artistic, political, and religious. In our lives, as the monk in his, we must become incarnational and institutional.

2. A second lesson we can learn from the Benedictine monastery is to create the regimen of a school in the Lord's service. Modern life is becoming a lifelong education. The Benedictine balance is magnificent—work, study, prayer. Can you suggest a better one? Work would include our vocation, our avocations, and our service to others. Here our burden of choice is terribly individual. The study should also be deliberately chosen. Most people never really "study" after their graduation from school. And the prayer should probably be far more formal and far more imaginative. Most Benedictine prayer was a chanting of the psalms. Do not imagine that you can abandon the simpler and more formal kinds of prayer. Be more "routine" in your reading of the psalms and in the memorizing and singing of hymns. As Samuel Johnson observed, "We need to be reminded more than we need to be instructed." But at the same time use these formal exercises in a free and easy way; "moving easy in harness" is Robert Frost's phrase. Rise above the words in wonder. But first of all create the tough-minded objective thrust of a school in the Lord's service.

3. A third lesson the Benedictine monks teach is a sense of the historical trajectory of Christian humility. Life is a river, and the apostolic experience of dying into life is now expressed as a simplicity of spirit. It has both dying and rising. The Benedictine monk is to live his whole life as if he were at a funeral. Life is to be a perpetual Lent. Bernard of Clairvaux, one of the greatest medieval teachers, is thoroughly Benedictine in writing: "Sinner that I am, my duty is not to teach but to mourn." [48] The spontaneity of apostolic daily dying has been transformed into the

[47] Nikos Kazantzakis, *The Rock Garden* (New York: Scribner's, 1963, p. 202.
[48] Coulton, *Five Centuries of Religion*, I, 300.

formal *miserere* sung by the cloister choir. This is clearly the trajectory of apostolic humility.

But note the person whose funeral they were attending—the Risen Lord. And so penitence was always to be followed by a celebration of resurrection rising. In a perpetual Lent they were always to look forward "with joy . . . to holy Easter." [49] The names given the monasteries suggest this: Good Place, Joyous Place, Dear Island, Sweet Vale, The Delights, Good Haven, Holy Valley, Sweet Fountain, The Resting Place, Abundance, and Joy. One of the representative and charming monastic stories demonstrates a simplicity of spirit, a peasant style of resurrection rising:

> "Let us have one quarrel like other men," said an old hermit who had lived for years in the same cell with another but without a disagreement. Quoth the other: "I do not know what a quarrel is like." Quoth the first: "We will put this brick between us, and each say 'It is mine,' then have a squabble over it." So they put the brick between them. "It is mine," said the first. "I hope it is mine," said the other. "If it is yours, take it," said the first—and so the poor attempt came to an end.[50]

This chapter began with Boris Pasternak and the question of how much we can do in the reshaping of life. Is it possible to create a form for dying and rising with Christ? William Butler Yeats, a traditionalist of the modern world, could have given Benedict words which answer *yes:*

> How but in custom and in ceremony
> Are innocence and beauty born?
> Ceremony's a name for the rich horn,
> And custom for the spreading laurel tree.[51]

---

[49] *Rule,* ch. 49, p. 65.
[50] Workman, *The Evolution of the Monastic Ideal,* pp. 350-51.
[51] William Butler Yeats, "A Prayer for My Daughter," *The Collected Poems of W. B. Yeats.* Copyright 1924 by The Macmillan Company, renewed 1952 by Bertha Georgie Yeats.

3 ❧ The Inwardness of the Mystic

> i thank You God for most this amazing
> day: for the leaping greenly spirits of trees
> and a blue true dream of sky;and for everything
> which is natural which is infinite which is yes
>
> (i who have died am alive again today,
> and this is the sun's birthday;this is the birth
> day of life and of love and wings:and of the gay
> great happening illimitably earth)
>
> how should tasting touching hearing seeing
> breathing any—lifted from the no
> of all nothing—human merely being
> doubt unimaginable You?
>
> (now the ears of my ears awake and
> now the eyes of my eyes are opened)
>   e. e. cummings [1]

We who are dead are alive again today in new forms of aliveness which say yes to everything which is natural. In this third chapter we shall explore how the mystic would go beyond the monk's outwardness to create an inward experience, not just as a renaissance of aliveness, but as an art form for dying into life.

Can We Shape a Subjective Style?

Yes, of course we can. Man creates the culture in which he lives, and a vast variety of life styles are not only possible but inevitable. No form is final, and each form must struggle for its own consistency, its own underlying unity. In Christian history it should be possible to shape a subjective style which continues the trajectory of both the apostle and the monk into the new day of the Renaissance.

We also live in a time of renaissance, and the style of life worked out by the mystics of the Spanish Renaissance should help us understand the expansion of life in the modern world. Both centuries, the sixteenth and the twentieth, have witnessed remarkable revolutions. In exploration, science, nationalism, secularism, and the growth of cities, there are striking parallels, but the significant revolution to note here is the reemergence of the subjective, the intuitive, the deeply personal. In both periods there was a breaking up of the forms of the past, whether medieval or Victorian, and a renewed interest in something deeper. There are differences too: the Spanish Renaissance searched for new life within Catholicism whereas our renaissance is said to be post-Christian. But the problems are parallel, and in the privatism, the cult of intimacy, and the sensitivity training of our day, a new mystic hopes to create an inward style of life that is believable.

This suggests the Renaissance problem. Can life, as it expands, still retain a sense of its limits? I have called these limits death, dying, doubt, despair, discipline: anything that serves as an act of collision and that conveys a sense of our human limitations. Can the Renaissance expansion of experience create a twofold vision, both a yes and a no, which makes a deeper life possible?

The Monk Becomes a Mystic

Christian mysticism developed very largely within medieval monasticism, and to understand the mystical style of life we must trace the development of Catholic history from Benedict in the early Middle Ages to John of the Cross in the late Renaissance.

In the sanctuary of the cloister the monk had chosen a simple life. Benedict had given him a discipline to follow. From the rising call for Matins until the closing chant of Compline his life was patterned. The time set aside for chapel services, devotional reading, and manual labor took over fourteen hours of his waking day, and yet it was still a simple rule for the governance of a man's whole life. Benedict had stayed close to his primary concern, the lifelong conversion of the individual monk; beyond this the *Rule* scarcely ventured. In an age of simple faith it would be enough.

The controlled environment of the monastery provided the objective expression the Catholic spirit needed. Within the bounds of its uncontrived simplicity the monk was free to work out his own life. He was given a simple but definite form, and it was up to him to invest it with spirit.

The Benedictine monastery was an expression of the spirit of the age, and in a time of turmoil and change it would be only natural for men to search for certainty and simplicity. The collapse of the Roman world drove men to reconstruct their lives in whatever patterns circumstances allowed, and the habits of one generation could last for centuries. One man, as a freeholder, would undertake a specific kind of service, and his son's son would recognize the obligation. This particularizing and objectifying tendency continued to characterize medieval society even after it attained a high culture. It was the medieval passion for outwardness. At a glance a peasant could recognize a priest or a monk, a page or a squire, a Venetian or a Florentine. The monk saw himself in a vast hierarchical order extending from the stones to the stars and through man to the choirs upon choirs of angels. The stability of his life style must have seemed eternal, but the whole Catholic culture was slowly changing. The poetic simplicity was giving way to organization and legalism. It was not just the great movements of monastic reform, Cluniac and Cistercian, nor even the proliferation of new forms, scholastic theologians and Franciscan friars, but the coming of a different spirit. The objective forms would not be lost, but the search would develop deeply interior forms of the religious life.

The directness and simplicity of the early Catholic mind was a beautiful achievement. It was not just ignorance and an unformed consciousness. In Augustine, for instance, we can see what it could do and what it preferred to leave undone. His way to God, like that of the early Middle Ages, was through revelation. He came to God through an experience in a garden, and thereafter he continued to seek God in the mystery of self-consciousness. This was directly in line with his early training in Neo-Platonism, which placed intuition above reason. The difference was that now he could claim that his personal experience corresponded directly to the creation before his eyes. He no longer lived in a shadow world; God has invested his intuition with an objective reality, and he was free to recognize the truth directly. In this he was more a searcher than a thinker, and in him speculation always stood below revelation. And yet he did not believe a man must choose either reason or revelation: he used both, and he established the threefold division of the mind—understanding, memory, and will—that we are to find later in John of the Cross. In all this Augustine was the great schoolmaster of the early medieval mind, and the life style he taught was informal, intuitive, and spontaneous. It was within the reach of all men—at any rate, all men who were trying seriously to lead a Christian life. There was no attempt to create a single coherent theological system. His biblical faith never allowed him to deify self-consciousness. It was this intuitive style, Platonic and existential, which dominated Catholic Christianity until the twelfth century.

In time and with the growth of the church a gradual change came over the medieval mind. The old poetic and intuitive emphasis was transformed as theologians struggled to interpret the faith. By the time of the Renaissance, reason had supplanted revelation as the major way to God. At first Anselm held to the past in arguing that man can only reason from the assumptions of revelation. Then Bernard, in debating Abelard, saw that faith could conflict with reason. The old Augustinian unity of reason and revelation began to split apart, and a new style of Christian life arose to champion reason. The scholastic theologian exalted reason as the best guide to truth, and this trend toward rationalism was encouraged by the reintroduction of Aristotle in Western Europe. His emphasis on the knowledge of the senses now took priority over Plato's intuition of unseen realities, and with Aristotle's help the high Middle Ages began to build a speculative theological system. This, of course, was the great achievement of Thomas Aquinas as he gave expression to the organizing principle of the medieval mind. Whereas early Christianity had emphasized the mystery of faith, the scholastics now stressed its rationality. Apostolic spontaneity and Benedictine simplicity, except among the first Franciscans, gave way to reason and the organizing genius of the late Middle Ages.

All through the Middle Ages there was an elaboration of religious forms which kept pace with the general cultural development. A climax was reached in the thirteenth century with Innocent III, Thomas Aquinas, Dante, Dominic, and Francis of Assisi, each pioneering a whole new series of developments. The medieval passion for outwardness was insatiable, and even the unknown was shaped and given form. Every saint was assigned a role with its attendant power, and when the saints were discredited, the craving for certainty created the cult of the guardian angel. Unfortunately this was soon followed by painful descriptions of death, purgatory, and hell. All of life was so saturated with religious imagery that it was becoming destructive. The ideas and images began to lose their meaning. In 1422 Henry V of England left money for twenty thousand requiem masses to be said for the repose of his soul. Henry Suso wrote of how he ate three quarters of an apple in the name of the Trinity and the remaining quarter in commemoration of the Virgin.[2] Corruption became common and contempt for the clergy grew. The papacy was made subservient to the French kings in the Babylonian Captivity, and its prestige was all but dissipated in the Great Schism with its two and then three bickering popes. The early brilliance of the Catholic organizing genius was fading into the rigid formalism of a waning culture. Between the dying of the Middle Ages and the birth of the Renaissance, the time was ready for the creation of a number of new life styles.

At least three major styles of life grew in response to the religious crisis of the sixteenth century. In the Protestant Reformation the break with the medieval church was an attempt to return to apostolic Christianity. Martin Luther created a tremendously intense style with a genuine dying into life. The pressure of the new age then forced the Catholic Church to institute its own Reformation, and in the Council of Trent the religion of the Middle Ages was reformed, defined, and given a legal finality. The church was Benedictine in the Middle Ages, but it became Jesuit after the Renaissance.[3] Ignatius Loyola represents the magnificently disciplined life style of the Catholic Reformation. I will show later why I do not think he taught a dying into life. A third style of life developed in the Carmelite cloister with Teresa

[2] J. Huizinga, *The Waning of the Middle Ages* (New York: Doubleday, Co. 1956), p. 152.
[3] Fernand Mourret, *A History of the Catholic Church* (St. Louis: B. Herder Book Co., 1930-1946), V, 612.

of Avila and John of the Cross. Its attempt was to retain the old medieval outwardness but to transcend it with the development of a new subjective experience of God. I believe it was an authentic expression of apostolic humility in the inward life of the mystic. The greater part of this chapter will be devoted to a study of John of the Cross.

Simple Mysticism Becomes Sophisticated

Mysticism has many meanings. In its simplest form it may be a sense of wonder, and in its highest development it may refer to union with God. One mistake that is commonly made is to identify the mystic with the psychic. Generally speaking, psychic research is concerned with the means (telepathy, clairvoyance, precognition) and mysticism with the ends (God, life, wonder). Some mystics seem to have no special psychic gifts, and many psychics have no mystical sense of life. I accept Cuthbert Butler's description of Augustine as my definition of mysticism: "Augustine is for me the Prince of Mystics, uniting in himself, in a manner I do not find in any other, the two elements of mystical experience, viz. the most penetrating intellectual vision into things divine, and a love of God that was a consuming passion." [4] Mysticism, then, is an art form which explores our sense of wonder as it is expressed in our knowledge of God and in our love of God. This art form has a history.

In the first twelve hundred years of Christian history we can trace mysticism from its simple, spontaneous beginnings to the development of a highly sophisticated contemplative theology. Paul's letters reveal a spontaneous mystical experience. In them there was no "mystic way," and all souls are open-windowed before the revelation of God. In the early church there was a tremendous sense of immediacy in the eschatological expectation of the coming of Christ. As this hope faded, a simple, direct sense of God's presence remained. An informal and spontaneous mysticism was characteristic of the early Middle Ages.

The mysticism of the early Middle Ages slowly developed out of this informal and intuitive experience. In the second century

[4] Butler, *Western Mysticism* (London: Constable, 1951), p. 20.

Clement of Alexandria wrote his *Miscellanies,* perhaps the first Christian treatise on mystical theology. The individual was to mortify all desire in order to rise to God in the emptiness of darkness. This was a negative simplicity. In the third century Plotinus, a Greek philosopher from Egypt, made Plato's thought available to the Middle Ages. He apparently did not believe in a personal God, but his Neo-Platonic thought helped establish guidelines for the future development of the mystical experience. His emphasis on intuitive experience, his understanding of the negative way, and his ladder of the mystical life were incorporated into medieval mysticism. Augustine was another pioneer in the art forms of mysticism. He distinguished the active and the contemplative lives, and then for the contemplative life he set up seven degrees of mystical development. In this early medieval emphasis the keynote was brevity and spontaneity. Benedict asked that prayer be "short and pure." And Pope Gregory believed that an individual might be able to pray for as long as half an hour at a time, but then the spirit is "beaten back" and sinks down by the weight of its own corruption.[5] In Bernard of Clairvaux, however, the early Platonic mysticism began to change. He was the last great champion of early mysticism in his passionate struggle for simplicity, but he was the first to speak of using images in contemplation to give expression to one's experience. He had unwittingly given his scholastic opponents a valuable tool, and the inner life was thrown open to organization. The simplicity of early Catholic mysticism could now become sophisticated.

The continuous development of a contemplative theology was now possible, and the new intellectual skills brought a change in direction. Aristotle's rational inquiry took precedence over Platonic intuition, and contemplative theology became scholastic. In one sense all medieval theologians are called scholastics, but in another sense the term is used to refer to the theologians from the twelfth or thirteenth century onward who make reason, and not intuition, the guiding principle in their thought. Thomas Aquinas provided the great scholastic synthesis, and with his systematic theology the mystics now had a beautifully defined in-

[5] John Chapman, "Mysticism," Hastings' *Encyclopedia of Religion and Ethics,* IX, 94.

tellectual tool for interpreting and enlarging their love of God. The two tracks, the mystical experience and the scholastic mind, worked together in scholastic mysticism. The mystic is always at his best when he combines "the warmth of his religious emotion" with "the luster of his intellect." [6]

The next development in Catholic mysticism lay with three schools of contemplation—German, Dutch, and Spanish. They all used two techniques in organizing the inner life: the negative way and scholastic (rational) thought. Mysticism now undertook a continuous development with the Germans in the fourteenth, the Dutch in the fifteenth, and the Spanish in the sixteenth centuries.

Meister Eckhart was the great figure in German mysticism. He wanted to promote "a complete fusion of man's nature with the nature of God." [7] The way to do this was negative; we are to "know nothing and want nothing." [8] If a man succeeds in this detachment, he will be rewarded with deification in God. Eckhart's words were extreme, his works were declared heretical, but his experience still continues to win a faithful following. Dag Hammarskjöld, the last figure in this study, was an admirer of Eckhart, and his words on the negative way stand as the first statement in *Markings:* "Only the hand that erases can write the true thing." [9]

German mystical idealism was a great inspiration to the more conventional mystics of the low countries in the next century. There Jan van Ruysbroek and the semi-monastic Brethren of the Common Life created a warmhearted devotional experience. Gerhard Groote and Thomas à Kempis captured its spirit in their charming little manual of ascetical exercises, *The Imitation of Christ*. Through its writing and teaching the Dutch school of mysticism was able to influence the new movements of the day. Erasmus, Luther, and Loyola attended their schools as children, and to an extent still to be determined this solid Dutch mysticism helped stimulate the third and perhaps greatest school of scholastic mysticism in Spain.

[6] Butler, *Western Mysticism,* p. 20.

[7] Arthur C. McGiffert, *A History of Christian Thought* (New York: Scribner's, 1932), II, 360.

[8] Pfeiffer, *Meister Eckhart* (1857), trans. C. de B. Evans (1924), p. 218, as quoted in *ibid.,* II, 372.

[9] Dag Hammarskjöld, *Markings* (New York: Alfred A. Knopf, 1964), p. 3.

Where the German was idealistic and the Dutch practical, the Spanish mystic was both deeply personal and highly formal—personal with the new Renaissance individuality and formal with the old spiritual formation of the Middle Ages. Teresa of Avila and John of the Cross are the best-known figures in Spanish mysticism, and I have chosen John of the Cross to represent the mystical experience of dying into life.

The choice was made for a number of reasons. First, John of the Cross lived in the great period of mysticism and at one of the few times when a person could be a mystic and only a mystic. He came at the height of a development that disintegrated rapidly in the next century. Second, I consider John's study of the mystical experience to be the most comprehensive we have. Third, his mystical experience parallels our theme of dying into life. There are also disadvantages. John of the Cross was so interior and so self-effacing that we cannot know all we would like about his life. Also, there are so many different kinds of mystics, and the deep and intense mysticism of John of the Cross does not represent the more cheerful and sweet-spirited mysticism of the Quaker. But it may just be that the sophisticated and comprehensive mysticism of the Spanish mystic can provide a framework for other equally valuable expressions of the mystical experience.

The Spanish Genius for Uniformity and Individuality

In the sixteenth century Spain experienced its Golden Age, the great century in the nation's history. In its exploration and conquest of the New World, in the political power of Charles V and Philip II, in its literary and artistic achievements, and in the vitality and discovery of its religious life, Spain led Catholic Europe in this period of the Renaissance.

The Golden Age came as the climax of a long development. A chaotic localism had come to characterize medieval Spain. Unlike France and English, Spain had not been able to build a stable society. The rugged terrain and the climate tended to separate communities and to encourage individualism. But with the final success of the Spanish crusade in 1492, eight long centuries of warfare against the Moors came to an end and national unity became a possibility. The Renaissance, coming at precisely this time, heightened the old individualism with a new belief in the dignity of man. Here there was no revolt against the forms of the past. The medieval church was scarcely challenged. New forms were simply added, and the culture was so enriched that in every area of activity Spanish civilization reached its highest expression. El Greco was painting in Toledo when Cervantes began to write in Seville. Don Quixote with all his idealism and Sancho Panza with all his earthy realism rode together in the conquest of the New World. It was a perfectly amazing cultural synthesis, and its spirit was reflected in its religion.

Religion was a major channel of national expression in the Spanish Renaissance. While six of Teresa's brothers sought their fortune as soldiers in the New World, she wore a flaming red dress the day she joined the convent in search of an inner kingdom. Neither she nor her brothers betrayed their background, for "there was no transition between the battlefield and the cloister." [10] Robert Sencourt estimates that one quarter of the Spanish people lived in religious houses,[11] and Gabriela Graham calculates that in Charles V's reign two-thirds of the lands of Spain were owned by the church.[12] Religion, surprisingly enough, was able to express both the uniformity and the individuality of the Spanish character. There are those extraordinary times in history when everyone wants to be an individual and every individual wants to go in the same direction.

Spanish religion was the dominant force in the Catholic Reformation, and the Jesuits were the officers. Ignatius Loyola, first a soldier for Spain and then a soldier for his Lord, created a military life style for the Christian faith. I find it fascinating but in many ways opposite to the theme of this book. The "Company of Jesus," as they first called themselves, created the supremely self-confident will and the fighting spirit of the soldier. This was to be subjected to a "cadaveric" obedience. If a Benedictine monk were ordered by his abbot to cross the Tiber in full storm, he would refuse to go if it threatened his life. No order that is out

[10] Gabriela Cunninghame Graham, *Santa Teresa* (London: A. and C. Black, 1894), I, 39.
[11] Robert Sencourt (Robert Esmonde Gordon George), *Carmelite and Poet* (New York: Macmillan, 1944), p. 124.
[12] Graham, *Santa Teresa*, I, 40.

of character with his vows should be obeyed. But if a Jesuit were commanded by the General of the Society, he would have to go because he would know that the responsibility belonged to his superior. This is not a feeling after life, or an intense dying into life, but a military style disguised, as Loyola so beautifully wrote, in which "the manner is ordinary." The Jesuits became the finest technologists of the new Catholic age. They were active mystics who could create their own visions through their *Spiritual Exercises,* not reactive mystics who must wait for grace. With over six hundred visions Loyola could boast that "I can find God at all times, whenever I will." [13] In our day the Society of Jesus is quite different; their intelligent humanism is no longer a training ground for a military spirit; but in the sixteenth century the Jesuits were able to be the leaders of the popular religion of the day, and in them the Spanish genius achieved a religious synthesis of unparalleled efficiency.

A deeper reach of the religious spirit was expressed in the Spanish mystics. Hernéndez y Pelayo believes that the writings of some three thousand mystics have survived from the Golden Age.[14] The mystical development took place in two waves. In the first half of the sixteenth century there was a wave of reform initiated by Cardinal Ximénez de Cisneros, and the emphasis was on ascetic discipline. Peter of Alcántara was such an ascetic. He made a compact with his body "that it should suffer on earth without intermission and after death be allowed to rest forever." [15] Tradition says that he did not lie down to sleep for fifteen years. When asceticism had cleared the ground with its reform, a second wave of insight arose. This movement can be characterized more by mystical gifts than with ascetic austerities, and the Carmelite Order provided the leadership. First known as a hermit community, then as the "White Friars" of a mendicant order, they came under the reforming zeal of Teresa of Avila. She led them back to the shoeless poverty of their early days. In one revolutionary step she added two hours of mental prayer to their daily regimen and thus made them "the order of mental prayer." The old dying

[13] René Fülöp-Miller, *The Power and Secret of the Jesuits* (New York: Viking Press, 1930), p. 4.
[14] E. Allison Peers, *Spanish Mysticism* (London: Methuen, 1924), p. 3.
[15] E. Allison Peers, *Spirit of Flame* (London: SCM Press, 1943), p. 88.

and rising of the apostle and the monastic outwardness of the monk were now to be matched by the inwardness of a mystical style of life.

A Conquistador of the Inner World

Within this background and at the very height of the Catholic Reformation, John of the Cross set up the successive stages of a mystical style of life. Trained in scholastic thought, he was able to work out the spiritual formation of a mystic way or, as Kierkegaard writes, "the inwardness of the mystic." In time Roman Catholicism recognized his work as the definitive study of the mystical life.

John was born in 1542 in the village of Pontiveros in Old Castille. His father was of a good family, but he was immediately disowned for marrying beneath his class. This forced him to turn to his wife's trade, weaving, in order to earn a living. Three sons were born to the struggling couple, but one died in infancy. When John was seven, his father died too, and his mother was forced to move to Arevalo to support the two children. There she placed John in the College of the Children of Doctrine, and he did well enough to secure a patron. From the age of fourteen to nineteen he was sponsored for the priesthood in one of the new Jesuit schools. A good mind and the gift of an education helped the boy rise out of a desperately insecure background.

Instead of joining the priesthood as he had been expected to do, John chose to become a Carmelite friar, and in 1563 he was admitted to the order at Medina. While studying at the University of Salamanca he met Teresa of Avila, the leader of Carmelite reform in Spain. She was fifty-two, and he twenty-five. Just five years earlier she had established the first convent for Discalced or Barefoot Carmelites, and she now persuaded John at their first meeting to help her found the first reformed house for men. From his graduation from Salamanca the following year John devoted the rest of his life to the reform movement within the Carmelite Order. He served as spiritual director, confessor, vicar, rector, prior, and finally counselor of a series of houses. His whole life was taken up in the work of the church.

Only two periods of storm broke the tranquillity of his life as a Carmelite friar. The first came when he was thirty-five. In the bitter dispute between the Calced and Discalced Carmelites ("with shoes" and "shoeless") over the problem of reform, the old order seized John and carried him off as a prisoner to the monastery at Toledo. There he was confined like a criminal to a little ten by six foot room. The rough cloak Teresa had given him was stripped off, his food was placed before him on the floor of the refectory, and he was scourged in the penance known to monasticism as the "circular discipline." The friars would walk around him in a circle, each striking him with a whip as he passed and handing it to the next in order.[16] All this he suffered in silence and even cheerfully. One night, after eight and one-half months in prison, he escaped by lowering himself from the outer wall of the monastery. This imprisonment provided the inspiration for almost all his poetry, and shortly after this he began to write his commentaries on the mystical life.

The other trial came at the end of John's life and this time at the hands of his own Carmelites. By 1588 he had risen in the Carmelite Order to become second-in-command to the vicar-general, Nicolás Doria. In 1591 Doria began to refashion the Reform according to his own ideas and against the constitution drawn up by Teresa in 1581. John of the Cross opposed his changes. The willful vicar-general then saw to it that John was not reelected to office. He was shorn of all power and returned to the ranks as a common friar. In a whispering campaign that was started to humiliate him further, he was "thrown into a corner like an old rag." [17] Yet neither in this crisis nor in his imprisonment did he allow himself to be embittered. But now in his exile at La Peñuela his health failed, septic poisoning set in, and he was still treated with little consideration. He died at the age of forty-nine, exhausted by his austere life and rejected, by and large, by the order he had helped to found. The records suggest that he died in the grand manner. The rain was falling outside when he told the friars gathered around him that he would sing Matins in Paradise.

A gracious spirit, not just in trial but in his daily life, was characteristic of John's temperament. He had the heart of one

[16] *Ibid.*, p. 39. [17] *Ibid.*, p. 75.

who had fallen in love. He was a small, unassuming person, just five feet two inches tall and gentle by nature. When he was moved to sympathy over the condition of a nun's robe, he begged in public for the means to buy her a new one. He was always extraordinarily solicitous for the sick. When a friar fell ill, he ordered the most expensive medicine for his relief. On his deathbed he called for the reading of the gentle Song of Songs. Underneath this graciousness there was an ascetic strength. This was the other side of his character. One story tells of how he whipped himself in public for breaking fast one evening and eating too early. He is said to have slept only two hours a night. He could be hard on others too when there was a purpose. When he learned that Teresa preferred to be served large hosts, he gave her a half of a host to help her mortify her desire. These two qualities, deep feeling and ascetic strength, are characteristic of the *caballeresco,* or cavalier, spirit of the Spanish saints of the sixteenth century.

In John of the Cross, as in Don Quixote, the cavalier Spanish spirit made for the loneliness of a strong, solitary individual. In his daily life he was closely yoked to the Carmelite friars, but he also had a deep need for privacy to sustain his interior life. He enjoyed arranging the altar for Mass or carving little wooden crucifixes. He also painted, and Teresa valued one of his paintings of Christ. Best of all he loved to spend time alone in nature: "When I am among the rocks I have fewer sins to confess than when I am among men." [18] Both Paul and Benedict spent years of their lives alone in the wilderness, whereas John was only able to spend an afternoon or a day by himself. This time apart meant a great deal to the mystic.

John's literary work, of course, provides our best guide to his mystical style of life. He is generally acclaimed one of the finest poets in the Spanish language, and the imprisonment at Toledo provided the inspiration for most of his poems. Using his poetry as scaffolding, he wrote four treatises as a complete survey of the contemplative life. All four must be considered a single, continuous process in which John has interpreted his own experience in the three traditional stages of the mystical life. In

[18] *The Complete Works of Saint John of the Cross* (Westminster, Md.: Newman Press, 1949), III, 361.

purgation, illumination, and union the believer is to progress from the natural state of sin to union with God. The first two commentaries, the *Ascent of Mount Carmel* and the *Dark Night of the Soul,* form a single work on ascetic mysticism. The last two, the *Spiritual Canticle* and the *Living Flame of Love,* describe the inflowing spiritual gifts. John did not intend to construct an exact pattern—the stages are all overlapping—but he hoped to provide a path by which a believer might know his experience and what he could do to complete his spiritual growth as a *conquistador* of the inner world.

The Ascetical Dying of the Mystic

The life style in John's mysticism is very obviously a reinterpretation of the Christian theme of dying into life. It is the apostolic experience of dying and rising with Jesus, and of the monastic school in the Lord's service, recast into the language of ascetical and mystical theology. In the language of mysticism the experience being hollowed out with denial is ascetical and the one expanding with spiritual gifts is mystical. The denial which Paul pictured as dying is now expressed as darkness, and the soul is to move toward God through a dark night of the soul.

In his two ascetical commentaries John traces a progressive development of self-denial. There are two major stages of purgation, one active and the other passive. The first commentary, the *Ascent of Mount Carmel,* presents the way in which an individual is to empty himself by his own efforts. The second, the *Dark Night of the Soul,* describes how he must remain passive as God completes his purification. Although these two stages are separated into the active and the passive night, they can also be thought of as occurring at the same time. It is usually considered convenient to treat them separately.

1. Active Denial in the Night of Sense

We are to begin by detaching ourselves from "every kind of pleasure which belongs to desire." [19] All our ties to natural things, even our love of beauty, goodness, and truth, are to be limited

[19] *Ibid.,* Vol. I, Bk. I, ch. III, 1, p. 21.

so that we can be free for the journey to God. This detachment is made possible through a process of self-denial:

> Strive always to choose, not that which is easiest,
>   but that which is most difficult, . . .
> Not that which gives most pleasure, but rather that
>   which gives least.[20]

This passage is often quoted to prove John a religious fanatic, and yet it is Jesus' call to repentance in the language of the scholastic mystic.

The Night of Sense calls for a painful detachment from life, but one can also see the hope that is held out for those who will undertake its denial. It leads to the fullest kind of possession:

> In order to arrive at having pleasure in everything,
>   Desire to have pleasure in nothing.
> In order to arrive at possessing everything,
>   Desire to possess nothing.[21]

2. Active Denial in the Night of Spirit

The Night of Sense is followed by the Night of Spirit. As we detached ourselves from our senses, we must also detach ourselves from everything that is spiritual. This insight is one of the peculiarly original touches in John of the Cross. We must actually deny our finest spiritual insights, even a vision from God, if we are to transcend ourselves. It is an active attack on all that we are, and once again it is painful.

Thus the soul must give up "that which it receives, either spiritually or sensually," [22] to pass beyond its own "natural limitations." [23] "In the night of sense there still remains some light, for the understanding and the reason remain. . . . But this spiritual night . . . deprives the soul of everything, both as to understanding and as to sense." [24] Like the German mystic the believer will enter a Cloud of Unknowing. This purgation must continue until

---

[20] *Ibid.,* Vol. I, Bk. I. ch. XIII, 5, p. 61.
[21] *Ibid.,* Vol. I, Bk. I, ch. XIII, 11, pp. 62-63.
[22] *Ibid.,* Vol. I, Bk. II, ch. IV, 6, p. 77.
[23] *Ibid.,* Vol. I, Bk. II, ch. IV, 5, p. 76.
[24] *Ibid.,* Vol. I, Bk. II, ch. I, 3, p. 68.

the soul is completely hollowed out by denial. Then in the emptiness of pure faith the seeker will find that "God dwells and is present substantially in every soul." [25]

John developed the Night of Spirit in a thoroughly scholastic fashion. The soul has three faculties—understanding, memory, and will. Each of these must be emptied in their own special way if they are to lead to union with God. Only the three theological virtues—faith, hope, and charity—can provide this union. Faith is to purge the understanding, hope the memory, and love the will. In this way, a way that may seem artificial to us, scholastic thought gave John of the Cross a means of organizing the mystical experience.

The key point to recognize is that John does not believe in what is usually meant by the orderly processes of religious growth. He does not believe that the natural self can be extended into the supernatural. Many, he says, "prefer feeding and clothing their natural selves with spiritual feelings and consolations, to stripping themselves of all things, and denying themselves all things for God's sake." [26] They are caught in a form of spiritual gluttony, for true spirituality consists in "the true annihilation of all sweetness in God." [27] The distance between God and man is infinite, and "there is no ladder whereby the understanding can attain to this high Lord." [28] Here, in the language of the scholastic mystic, is Luther's "by faith alone" and Kierkegaard's "leap of faith."

In the Night of Spirit John is trying to correct the popular mysticism of his day. Some fifty years earlier Ignatius Loyola had created a ladder "to lead man to the highest goal with the aid of his natural capacities and senses." [29] In his own life he "disciplined and trained his power of imagination in the school of contemplative prayer so that it obeyed instantly, and permitted him to experience visions, illuminations, and visitations whenever he desired." [30] A typical Jesuit meditation was the saying of the

[25] *Ibid.*, Vol. I, Bk. II, ch. V, 3, p. 79.
[26] *Ibid.*, Vol. I, Bk. II, ch. VII, 5, p. 89.   [27] *Ibid.*
[28] *Ibid.*, Vol. I, Bk. II, ch. VIII, 7, p. 98.
[29] Fülöp-Miller, *The Power and Secret of the Jesuits*, p. 6.
[30] Heinrich Boehmer, *The Jesuits* (Philadelphia: Castle Press, 1928), p. 37.

Lord's Prayer, one breath for each word, and praying the words slowly while imagining oneself at the foot of the cross, in the rain, spattered with blood, with the cursing of soldiers and the shock of the earthquake. Against this John wrote that all our visions, revelations, locutions, interior feelings, and all kinds of spiritual operations are imperfect channels for God's grace. There is "no mode or manner" [31] which can unite the soul directly to God. We must undertake a Night of the Spirit.

Up to this point discursive meditation provided the chief means of denial and detachment. There comes a time, however, when a person must lay aside this active work if he is to continue the journey of faith. John gives three signs to help the believer determine when that time has come. The first is when he no longer enjoys meditation, the second is when he has no desire to fix his meditation on a particular object, and the third is when he takes pleasure in waiting on God in simplicity and silence. Then one must give up active meditation for the deeper state of contemplation.

3. Passive Denial in the Night of Sense

In his second book, *The Dark Night of the Soul,* John of the Cross describes the experience of contemplation in which God purifies the soul in a state of passivity. In this stage we must wait upon God in simplicity and silence. Once again the night can be divided into a Night of Sense and a Night of Spirit. The first is "bitter and terrible to the sense," and "the second bears no comparison with it, for it is horrible and awful to the spirit." [32]

An individual may know that he is in the passive Night of Sense when three conditions are true. He will find no pleasure in either spiritual or created things, he will continually think of God, and yet a disciplined meditation is impossible. The thing to do is "to remain in peace and quietness." [33] It will seem like a waste of time, but one is to trust that God will do the active work.

[31] *Complete Works of Saint John of the Cross,* Vol. I, Bk. II, ch. XVI, 7, p. 133.
[32] *Ibid.,* Vol. I, Bk. I, ch. VIII, 2, p. 371.
[33] *Ibid.,* Vol. I, Bk. I, ch. X, 4, p. 379.

4. Passive Denial in the Night of Spirit

The most painful experience of all comes at this stage of the "dark night of the soul." The denial has now gone so far that one cannot even pray; all the old forms of life have fallen away and one is empty before God. It is a surprising state because one would have imagined, at this mature level of spiritual development, that life's suffering was gone. And yet Christian saints —Luther, Pascal, Tolstoi, Simone Weil—all testify to the reality of the dark night of the soul. It teaches us once again, but on a much deeper level of experience, that life contains a dying experience.

John of the Cross presents this final stage of purgation as the purification of a furnace. There are "intervals of relief," but like a log in the fire we are made "dry, . . . black, . . . and finally kindled and transformed . . . as beautiful as fire." [34] What he calls "the dark fire of love has assailed us," [35] but in order to enkindle us as a living flame of love. Secretly and unknown to us at first, God's spirit is beginning to quicken our lives. The emptiness continues, but the soul is entering a new phase of growth known as "infused contemplation." [36] Spiritual blessings begin to come. The first are negative. The knowledge of oneself and one's misery. But other positive ones follow. Virtue can now be practiced. God will continue to send trials to purify one's life, but the time will come when the soul is ready "to soar upward to its God along the road of solitude." [37] Now it is a "happy night." In the two mystical commentaries that follow, John enters a life of love in which faith is the marriage of God and the soul.

An Interpretation of His Asceticism

The usual charge brought against John of the Cross is that he was too severe in his demand for self-denial. Dean Inge believes that he "carried self-abnegation to a fanatical extreme, and presents the life of holiness in a grim and repellent spirit." [38] Even those

---

[34] *Ibid.*, Vol. I, Bk. II, ch. XXIV, 1, p. 429.

[35] *Ibid.*, Vol. I, Bk. II, ch. XI, 7, p. 436.

[36] *Ibid.*, Vol. I, Bk. I, ch. XIV, 1, p. 394.

[37] *Ibid.*, Vol. I, Bk. II, ch. XXV, 4, pp. 485-86.

[38] Inge, *Christian Mysticism*, p. 223.

who appreciate his contribution are forced to admit that he was a hard saint.

John did call for severe denial, but it was not his intention to destroy human individuality. We have already shown that in his own life he preserved a strong sense of integrity. His intention was to deny the natural operations of the senses and the spirit, but in order to fulfill them on a higher level. His highest state, as it was with Teresa, is one in which the mystic is returned to life in the world.

John's ascetical writings do convey a sense of annihilation. In judging one of his works Teresa wrote: "It would be bad business for us if we could not seek God until we are dead to the world." [39] A literal following of his teachings might lead a novice into serious psychological difficulties. John asks him to hold back "nothing, nothing, nothing, till one's very skin and all the rest is lost for Christ." [40] I think what saves John himself from the annihilation of his personal integrity is his indestructible Spanish individuality and a characteristic exaggeration in his style of writing and thinking. We see this in our day in Miguel de Unamuno: "The real sin . . . is the sin of heresy, the sin of thinking for oneself." [41] No matter how severe these Spaniards seem to be with themselves, and no matter what they write, they manage to survive and to allow nothing to annihilate their integrity.

The more serious criticism is that John's asceticism cut him off from the world. Again this was not his intention. He was not looking for any kind of experience, whether like Zen *satori* or Hindu *samadhi,* which is above the ordinary daily experience. But he was out of touch with much of the life of the world. Within himself he created a private experience, a mystic way. Teresa saw this danger in John when she wrote: "God deliver me from people who are so spiritual that they want to turn everything into perfect contemplation, come what may." [42] Protestants tend to set up systems of salvation whereas Catholics erect ladders of perfec-

[39] *The Compete Works of Saint Teresa of Avila* (New York: Sheed and Ward, 1945), III, 267.

[40] Jacques Maritain, *The Degrees of Knowledge* (New York: Scribner's, 1938), p. 406.

[41] Unamuno, *The Tragic Sense of Life,* pp. 71-72.

[42] *Complete Works of Saint Teresa of Avila,* III, 267.

tion. And both have the danger of privatism. This criticism is particularly appropriate of the scholastic mystic. The mystic, if he is only a mystic, does cut himself off, not necessarily from the world, but in a very specialized experience. John was undoubtedly a specialist, but in the art form of mysticism he worked out a comprehensive and wonderfully sensitive progression of the inner life.

The Mystical Rising of the Ascetic

John's two mystical commentaries describe the mystical gifts that flow into the ascetical experience. The *Spiritual Canticle* traces the stages of his growth in grace, and the *Living Flame of Love* explains more fully the final plateau of experience in the mystical style of life.

The *Spiritual Canticle,* then, sets forth three successive stages in the mystical life—love, spiritual betrothal, and spiritual marriage. An undertone of suffering and denial continues throughout the mystical life, but the gifts that are received come in these three stages.

The first mystical stage brings a taste of God's love, and by love John meant an affectionate bond binding us to God. As the soul is hollowed out, it is gradually infused with new life. Three kinds of pain describe the way in which God's love comes into the soul—the sense of a wound, a sore, and dying. Each one deepens the soul's sense of need and its capacity for receiving the gift of love. For brief times the soul may rise above the body and its pain, but these will not last, and the individual will need to grow into a deeper and more continuous experience of communion.

In the second stage, spiritual betrothal, the soul attains a far steadier sense of God's love. The bond of spiritual marriage has not been completed, but there is now a definite promise of union with God. The soul gains a sense of recollectedness and self-mastery, a new sense of spiritual sureness. A movement of passivity sets in, and from here on the individual should try simply to wait before God.

The third stage, spiritual marriage, is a state of union with God, a plateau of love in which we know that God is always present. John's long ascetical training now prompts him to say that suffering continues but the pain is gone! In some way God stands at the center of the soul, and our will is converted in the will of God. The life of tension still continues, individuality is not destroyed, but John claims to have reached his goal of union with God.

In the *Living Flame of Love,* the second mystical commentary, John expands his description of this final stage in the mystical experience. "Union with God" is not an easy phrase to understand. It is meant to signify a union of man's will with the will of God. This is possible, John believed, because God stands at the center of the soul. Deep within the soul the union is so complete that the individual cannot tell where God's light begins and his own ends. This is not to say that all the distinctions between God and man have ended. John is careful to avoid a heretical position. The soul is divine in its operations but not in its essence. The soul is transformed into God "by participation" but not in its "substance." The life of tension continues, man's individuality is not destroyed, but he has come alive with love.

An Interpretation of His Mysticism

John of the Cross was both a mystic and a scholastic. I am attracted by his mystical insights but not by his scholastic way of organizing his experience.

John's scholasticism allowed him to organize a coherent mystical style of life. Reason, not intuition, was the major faculty in medieval scholasticism. And John was typically medieval in his praise of reason. He wrote: "[The] most inward part, which is the rational part . . . has a capacity for community with God." [43] A second assumption he made was that the deepest areas of the subjective life are in some way closed to evil, "where neither the devil nor the world nor sense can enter." [44] With a faith in reason and a deification of the inner consciousness he could build a mystical system. He had isolated a part of his total experience and then held it up to God for sanctification. Much mystical experience, however, is not nearly so manageable. In George Fox

[43] *Complete Works of Saint John of the Cross,* Vol. II, stanza XXXI, 4, p. 154.
[44] *Ibid.,* Vol. III, stanza I, 9, p. 23.

and in William Blake it is often wild and unpredictable and just as rewarding. The psychological sciences and the study of comparative religions have enormously enlarged the religious consciousness, and no modern mysticism can hope to integrate the mystical experience as John sought to do in his day. But scholasticism was already being discredited in the sixteenth century, and John had chosen a way of thinking which was too rationalistic and too inflexible to do justice to his own mystical experience.

The real appeal of John's mysticism is not its system, nor his own life, about which we know too little, but the insights with which he describes and directs his reader's experience. He was a great spiritual director. Here I concur with his translator and biographer, E. Allison Peers, that John of the Cross is "the greatest psychologist in the history of mysticism." [45] His literary style is crystal clear and eminently logical. With twenty short quotations, taken progressively through his books, I would suggest his deeply personal appeal:

1. No man of himself can succeed in voiding himself of all his desires in order to come to God. [46]

2. Love creates a likeness between that which loves and that which is loved. [47]

3. All the virtues increase by the practice of any of them, and all the vices increase by the practice of any one of them likewise. [48]

4. The soul must be in darkness in order to have light for the road. [49]

5. A soul must pass beyond everything to unknowing. [50]

6. I am appalled . . . when some soul with the very smallest experience of meditation . . . [says] . . . "God said to me . . ."; "God answered me . . ."; whereas it is not so at all, but, as we have said, it is for the most part they who are saying it to themselves. [51]

7. Meditation is the work of the soul, and God is the

[45] Peers, "General Introduction," *ibid.,* Vol. I, xl.
[46] *Ibid.,* Vol. I, Bk. I, ch. I, 5, p. 19.
[47] *Ibid.,* Vol. I, Bk. I, ch. IV, 3, p. 24.
[48] *Ibid.,* Vol. I, Bk. I. ch. XII, 5, p. 58.
[49] *Ibid.,* Vol. I, Bk. II, ch. III, 6, p. 73.
[50] *Ibid.,* Vol. I, Bk. II, ch. IV, 4, p. 76.
[51] *Ibid.,* Vol. I, Bk. II, ch. XXIX, 4, p. 210.

spectator of that work—contemplation is the work of God, and the soul is the spectator of that work.[52]

8. Wherefore it is better to learn to silence the faculties and to cause them to be still, so that God may speak.[53]

9. All possession is contrary to hope.[54]

10. For the troubles and disturbances which are bred in the soul by adversity are of no use or profits for bringing prosperity; indeed, as a rule, they make things worse and also harm the soul itself.[55]

11. Patience is a surer sign of the apostolic man than the resuscitation of the dead.[56]

12. Spiritual persons suffer great trials, by reason not so much of the aridities which they suffer, as of the fear which they have of being lost on the road, thinking that all spiritual blessing is over from them and that God has abandoned them.[57]

13. And where there is no love, put love. And you will find love.[58]

14. God visits the soul, wounding it and upraising it in love, He is wont to bestow on it certain enkindling touches of love, which like a fiery arrow strike and pierce the soul and leave it wholly cauterized with the fire of love.[59]

15. All that I do I do through love, and all that I suffer I suffer for love's sake.[60]

16. The winter is now past and the rain has gone and the flowers have appeared upon our earth.[61]

17. The soul that is secure and peaceful is like a continual feast.[62] [John's biographers say that "as he walked along he would tap the walls with his knuckles to make sure he was still on earth." [63]]

[52] J. G. Bennett, *Christian Mysticism and Subud* (New York: Dharma Book Co., 1961), p. 14.
[53] *Complete Works of Saint John of the Cross*, Vol. I, Bk. III, ch. III, 4, p. 235.
[54] *Ibid.*, Vol. I, Bk. III, ch. VII, 2, p. 241.
[55] *Ibid.*, Vol. I, Bk. III, ch. VI, 3, p. 240.
[56] *Ibid.*, Vol. III, Spiritual Sayings, Ninth Saying, p. 313.
[57] *Ibid.*, Vol. I, Bk. I, ch. X, 1, p. 378.
[58] I cannot locate this.
[59] *Ibid.*, Vol. II, stanza I, 9, pp. 34-35.
[60] *Ibid.*, Vol. II, stanza XIX, 7, p. 113.
[61] *Ibid.*, Vol. II, stanza XXVII, 6, p. 143.
[62] *Ibid.*, Vol. II, stanzas XXIX and XXX, 8, p. 151.
[63] Elizabeth Hamilton, *Saint Teresa* (New York: Scribner's, 1959), p. 166.

18. The soul gradually acquires virtues and strength and perfection, together with bitterness, for virtue is made perfect in weakness, and is wrought by the experience of sufferings.[64]

19. The soul in this state must bear in mind that, although it is not conscious of making any progress, it is making much more than when it was walking on foot.[65]

20. Oh, how happy is this soul that is ever conscious of God.[66] [Teresa is reputed to have said: "You can't speak about God to John of the Cross because he goes into an ecstacy and makes others do the same." [67]]

In these words John of the Cross counsels the development of an inwardness that is surprisingly attractive to the private nihilistic experience of modern life. In his book on *The Experience of Nothingness,* Michael Novak addresses John's message to the revolutionary young-adult generation: "The myth appropriate to the new time requires a constant return to inner solitude, an unbroken awareness of the emptiness at the heart of consciousness." [68] This is an emptiness which John believed could be filled with God, and this may help explain why mysticism is making a resurgence today.

Growth Without Gluttony

Both the Middle Ages and the Renaissance shaped the mystical experience of John of the Cross. His ascetical dying came from the medieval *via negativa,* but now the outward forms are made intensely personal and carried inward. The enormous expansion of experience which was the Renaissance was reflected in the mystical rising of his gentle love and his cavalier poetry. It was a new style of life and a new, deeply interior expression of dying and rising with Christ.

The modern world is turning toward the intuitive, the introspective, the interior life. "Consciousness," Emily Dickinson wrote, "is the only home we *now* have." [69] The question is whether the

[64] *Complete Works of Saint John of the Cross,* Vol. III, stanza II, 22, p. 51.

[65] *Ibid.,* Vol. III, stanza III, 58, p. 95.

[66] *Ibid.,* Vol. III, stanza IV, 15, p. 112.   [67] Hamilton, *Saint Teresa,* p. 53.

[68] Novak, *The Experience of Nothingness* (New York: Harper, 1970), p. 116.

[69] Richard Chase, *Emily Dickinson* (New York: Dell Publishing Co., 1965), p. 182.

modern renaissance can manage to maintain the limits of life in all its new forms of experience—its art and entertainment, its Yoga and Zen, its drugs and sensitivity training, and all the ways in which consciousness is expanding. A life-giving experience without a recognition of the limits of life will turn us, as John of the Cross warned, into "spiritual gluttons," and a hedonistic culture can become empty and demonic. The present search seems to be for a personal and somewhat private life style, and the next step may be a more widespread re-creation of community life styles. Mysticism may prove to be a helpful art form in creating and maintaining the intuitive and imaginative dimension of modern life.

No mystic in the modern world has been more interesting than Albert Schweitzer, and he demonstrates the dimensions of the mystical experience. His life style focused on the phrase "reverence for life," words that came to him as he was moving upstream through a herd of hippopotamus. His mystical reverence moved on three levels—nature mysticism, a fellowship with those who suffer, and the dying and rising of the Lord Jesus.

The life of mystical communion can now move through a great many art forms. Thoreau believed that "we need to witness our own limits transgressed, and some life pasturing freely where we never wander." [70] For some Bach is the fifth evangelist, and his chorales are communion. But some will want to work on the experinece directly, and shape new mystical styles for the modern mind. John of the Cross gives us guidelines which we will need to follow in any mystical style which is Christian:

> Our mystical experience must have the two halves of ascetism and mysticism. The dying of asceticism will be life-long, and even the spiritually mature must learn to live with the dark night of the soul. The moments of ecstacy which we should all have on occasion need no longer be episodic, and we can hope to have an ongoing sense of the presence of God.

Most of the time I feel that I am a Platonic and Augustinian mystic of the early Middle Ages. My gifts are short and simple and spontaneous. But John arranges them in order and gives me a sense of direction. Think about this in your own experience.

---

[70] Henry Thoreau, *Walden* in *The Portable Thoreau* (New York: Viking Press, 1957), p. 557.

4 ✺ The Last Puritan
and the First Pietist

Art is always the result of some kind of restraint. . . .
Every time it feels vigorous, it looks for a struggle and an
obstacle. It loves to burst its sheaths and so it chooses them
tight. Is it not in periods when life is overflowing that
the need of the strictest forms torments the great heroic
geniuses? Hence the use of the sonnet during the luxuriant
Renaissance by Shakespeare, Ronsard, Petrarch, and even
Michelangelo; the use of the *terza rima* by Dante; the love
of the fugue in Bach; that restless need of the constraint
of the fugue in the last works of Beethoven. . . .

The great artist is one whom constraint exalts, for whom
the obstacle is a springboard. It was to a defect in the
marble, they tell us, that Michelangelo owed the massed
tension in the gestures of his Moses. . . . Art is born of
constraint, lives on struggle, dies of freedom.

André Gide[1]

Religion is the art form of life. Through discipline we learn to
be free, through dying we move forward into life. In this chapter
we shall present a Christian archetype, the Puritan and the Pietist,
in his struggle to unite outwardness and inwardness into a life
style in the modern world.

A Secret Discipline and a Holy Worldliness

The Renaissance, not the Reformation, sets the tone for the
modern world, and our experience continues to expand at an increasing rate. One of the major problems is how we are to achieve
integration when the options are endless. Shall we become cultic and
force closure, or are we to be endlessly open but lose our identity?
Is there a style in which we can open up to new experiences in
the arts, in travel, in education, in entertainment, and then center down on the achievement of an integrity which means responsibility, study, service? In this crisis some people choose

[1] André Gide, *Pretexts: Reflections on Literature and Morality* (London:
Meridian Books, 1959), pp. 63-64.

premature closure; they close themselves off from new forms of life. Other people remain open, but so open that they lose the integration which makes for integrity. It is difficult to do both: to open up and to center down.

A Christian style for the modern world must be able to hold life's opposites together in a complex personality. The three archetypes presented thus far were chosen as illustrations of different styles of dying into life, but whereas the apostle lived out in the world, the monk and the mystic achieved their synthesis in the controlled environment of the cloister. In our day the modern Christian must bring together life's opposites (life and death) in the midst of the world. Eberhard Bethge suggests that it will take both discipline and worldliness: "Secret discipline without worldliness becomes pure ghetto; worldliness without the secret discipline pure boulevard." [2] Not the boulevard of the world nor the ghetto of the cloister, but a synthesis which is a holy worldliness is now needed.

In the eighteenth century John Wesley worked out a style which could carry a disciplined religious experience into the life of the world. He brought together Puritan asceticism and Pietist mysticism; in his Puritan discipline he discovered a Pietist joy, and it was a portable style that could catch the hearts of thousands of converts in the English world. We will begin with his historical background.

Martin Luther as the First Modern Man

Psychoanalytic theory recognizes the Renaissance as the great ego revolution, and its energy could move in opposite directions. In Spain, John of the Cross used it to refine medieval mysticism whereas in Germany, Luther broke out of the monasticism and mysticism of the past to create the consciousness of modern man. It was not his intention. Luther became a monk, he greatly admired the mystics, and he tried to express his bursting opposites within the old forms. But it was not possible for him, nor was it possible for Germany. The medieval tradition of dying was too somber, too melancholy, too tightly restricted for the spirit of

[2] Mary Bosanquet, *The Life and Death of Dietrich Bonhoeffer* (New York: Harper, 1968), p. 280.

the new age, and Luther discovered this within himself. The whole range of his experience was available to him, and in this he became the man of the future. In his experience were the elements for new emerging styles of life.

Luther still lived out of the central paradox of dying into life, but he learned how to unite the polarities of life and death in a new way. His exuberant emphasis on life is universally recognized, but there is also much of what we have called dying in his experience. He was a sad youth who had lost his childhood: "I did not know the Christchild any more." [3] As a monk he was a sick young man overcome with despair: "I was holy. I killed nobody but myself." [4] He worked the penitential system, he confessed every intention as well as every deed; but he was now tormented with his own scrupulosity. His goal, of course, was God. As Nietzsche wrote, "Luther wanted to speak to God directly, speak as himself, and without embarrassment." [5] But he was overwhelmed with dying, and he found no peace.

So within monasticism Luther turned toward mysticism, and the vicar of the Augustinian order, at this time Luther's best friend, Johann von Staupitz, was a mystic. But mysticism for Luther (as for many of us) was to remain a very mixed experience. Moments of grace, yes. Its goal in God, again yes. But Luther could not become passive before God. Not all of him anyway. And yet he kept alive the great opposites with which the mystic wrestled. His emphasis on asceticism never left him. Sometimes he called it dying: "In the midst of death we live." [6] Sometimes this dying is from the devil, but more often he sees death as a process through which God leads us to life: "Whom he would make alive he must first kill." [7] But it is not in the cloister, nor before the altar, that this must happen. It is a constant cross which we bear all through life. Occasional failure is better than a perfect record because it leads to humility. In all this Luther has preserved the polarities of his past, but he has cast the struggle out into the world.

[3] Erik H. Erikson, *Young Man Luther* (New York: W. W. Norton and Co., 1958), p. 119.

[4] *Ibid.*, p. 109. [5] *Ibid.*, p. 97.

[6] Ronald H. Bainton, *Here I Stand* (Nashville: Abingdon Press, 1950), p. 370.

[7] *Ibid.*, p 82.

Out in the world our sense of God tends to become evangelical rather than mystical. Both words are very much alike: both suggest the experience of God's presence; both deal with feelings. But whereas mysticism is closer to Jesus' incarnation, evangelicalism is closer to our redemption through Christ on the cross. Maybe it is John's Gospel versus Paul's letters. But Luther is Pauline; he is the historical man; he experiences moments in time. Before his conversion death had power over him, body and soul:

> In devils's dungeon chained I lay
> The pangs of death swept o'er me.[8]

But now, in a moment of time, and in reading Paul's Epistle to the Romans: "Thereupon I felt myself to be reborn and to have gone through open doors into paradise." [9] The new Protestant life styles will continue to know life and death, but Luther had begun to recast the polarities into an evangelical pattern. We shall shape our style in the world, and we shall meet God in the crises of time. The struggle, of course, will still be lifelong, but it will not achieve the Benedictine peace of God or the Carmelite union with God. "Faith," Luther wrote, "is a living, restless thing." [10]

Luther defined the guidelines, but not the life style, of the Protestant future. Like Paul he was too active in his rebellion against the past to be free to create a settled style. And Luther in his later years needed the definition of a stabilizing style. It is very difficult in any art form to maintain one's creativity, and Kierkegaard suggested that the old Luther needed a martyr's death. But for richness of insight he was unparalleled since Augustine, and in his willingness to work on the frontiers of consciousness he opened up a new world for modern man. Today, in this vastly inclusive modern life, most of us will need a more sharply defined life style if we are to live with integrity.

The Reformer Becomes a Puritan

The Reformation rapidly moved forward in the spiritual formation of new life styles. Lutheranism and Calvinism were the

[8] *Ibid.*, p. 66.   [9] *Ibid.*, p. 65.   [10] *Ibid.*, p. 331.

two major forms of Protestantism; there were some things they had in common and some things in which they were opposite. Both placed a high emphasis on the individual; both called for a personal relationship with God. Lutheranism, however, internalized its style and, like Luther, wrestled with the inner life. It rejected self-discipline as simply a new form of the old Catholicism, and it called for a deep-seated Christian humility. At its worst Lutheranism could become passive, but at its best the Word of God could create an experience of forgiveness. Calvinism, on the other hand, pointed its interest outward. In the fear of God it developed new objective forms of expression—a disciplined Christian man and a Puritan commonwealth. The Calvinist style of Christianity best suited the English temperament.

In England the new spirit of the Reformation began to work within the Establishment. The nation had been a unity since the Middle Ages, and under Henry VIII and Queen Elizabeth the people went through the Reformation together. A middle way was created out of the medieval emphasis on reason and the Renaissance emphasis on experience. A rational empiricism has characterized England until the present day. "Passion" may be the great word for the Spanish, "thought" for the French, but the English (and the Americans) have always believed that "action" speaks louder than words and feelings and ideas.[11] In the seventeenth century the developing English spirit went Puritan.

Puritanism is an effort to exernalize the experience of salvation. God is infinitely high: "The Calvinist God may be a tyrant, but he is not corruptible with bribes." [12] Man is infinitely low: "In Adam's fall we sinned all." [13] Only the grace of God can bring the two together. Repentance, conversion, and rebirth is the way. And it is God alone who predestines whether we are to be saved or lost. There is inner experience, of course. The Puritans knew an inward gladness and a source of inexhaustible delight, but the emphasis was more on the knowing than on the feeling. The one

---

[11] Salvador de Madariaga, *Englishmen, Frenchmen, Spaniards* (New York: Hill and Wang, 1969).

[12] Preserved Smith, *The Age of the Reformation* (New York: Henry Holt and Co., 1920).

[13] "The Alphabet in the New England Primer," in *American Poetry and Prose,* ed. Norman Foerster (Boston: Houghton Mifflin, 1934), p. 49.

absolute beatitude was the universal knowledge of regeneration. You belonged, you were God's elect. For a sense of this grace the saints would scrutinize their souls each day. They drew up resolutions, they kept journals. Their experience, of course, was broader than their religion. The Puritans were people of great gusto. They never condemned desire, only the abuse of it. "God," they said, "has given us temporals to enjoy, . . . food, love, music, study." [14] But for all their humanity they were a somber people. To have purity of heart is to seek one thing. Puritans did just that, and it was around this Puritan singleness of heart that they built their lives, their families, and their communities. The way to heaven, they said, lies through hostile country full of ambushes, and you must dispute every step at sword's point. Great faith, great energy, and like Emily Dickinson's grandfather they "believed like fury." [15] The deeply self-conscious, introspective Puritan mind was ascetical far more than it was mystical. You needed to pray for the repentance of your repentance and then to beg God's pardon for all your prayers. It externalized its faith, even its personal faith, and it did this with the whole world as its monastery.

Why did the Puritan life style fail? It would seem to have survival value in today's Good Friday world. It failed because it was too intense; it was too intense for its children and its grandchildren. It failed because it hardened into dogma. Santayana spoke of himself as a Puritan "in the long arctic night of the nordic." [16] It failed because the world changed and the Renaissance crowded out the Reformation. We seized upon the perfectibility of man's goodness, and forgot about the perfectibility of evil. For some, of course, Puritanism never failed. John Donne used the Puritan style to bind life's opposites together into what he called an "evenness" within himself. But the Puritans would have cared most, not for the experience they created, but for the Christ they found. Their emphasis was objective. Below John Donne's statue in St. Paul's Cathedral the words point outward: "He watches for him whose name is Light." Two centuries later

[14] Perry Miller, *The New England Mind* (New York: Macmillan, 1939), p. 41.

[15] Chase, *Emily Dickinson,* p. 10.

[16] George Santayana, *The Last Puritan* (New York: Scribner's, 1936).

Emily Dickinson wept for the lost Puritan style of life as the day "Heaven died." [17]

Each new life style is carried forward in the forms of its successor. Puritanism lived on in Pietism. The Age of Reason dominated the seventeenth and eighteenth centuries, and Puritanism was one form of its expression. By the middle of the eighteenth century first Rousseau and later the English poets were ushering in Romanticism, an Age of Sentiment. Reason and emotion were splitting apart. In Moravian Pietism, Luther's personal feeling at last crossed over to England from Germany. The Puritans, of course, had feelings and the Pietists had reason. But it does help to speak of Puritan outwardness and objectivity, and the Pietist emphasis on the inner life. At the time, however, when these two movements were overlapping, it was possible to begin as a Puritan and then to become a Pietist. Jonathan Edwards, America's great Puritan preacher, was just such a man. John Wesley, since he was so powerful in helping England make the transition between these two movements, might be called the last Puritan and the first Pietist.

The Last Puritan and the First Pietist

John Wesley was born in 1703 in the rectory of the Church of England at Epworth. His was a remarkably religious family. Samuel Wesley was the third in a line of ministers, and his wife, Susanna, was the daughter of a prominent Puritan preacher. The eight of their nineteen children that reached maturity always remained faithful to the church, and their three sons became ministers of the Church of England. For the Wesley family, as Alfred North Whitehead observed of the church in his father's day, "the Church was the nation rising to the height of its civilization." [18]

The family meant more in the eighteenth century than it does today, and John Wesley's parents were magnificent educators and spiritual directors. The Rev. Samuel Wesley was a thoroughly likable person, a hopeful scholar who never succeeded in securing the recognition and advancement he wanted, and an outspoken,

[17] Chase, *Emily Dickinson*, p. 62.
[18] Whitehead, *Science and Philosophy* (New York: Philosophical Library, 1948), p. 28.

stubborn, but faithful parish priest. His gift to his fifteenth child, John, was love, patience in trial, and a passion for the things of the mind. His greatest gift was as a person whom his children could respect.

The mother, Susanna Wesley, is deservedly one of the great women in the religious heritage we all share. Samuel maintained careful records of the household expenses, but Susanna created an all-encompassing system for the governance and education of the family. Her central idea was to set times and limits for everything. Except for instruction in ancient languages the father left the family to the mother to discipline and educate. She taught them how to "cry softly," she allowed no eating between meals, and family prayers were at 6:00 P.M., just before supper. She taught them manners, and she trained their minds. From nine to twelve and from two to five she ran her own school in the Lord's service. She was the teacher, and in her classroom she taught reading, sewing, biblical instruction, and whatever a child should know. And then once a week, with each child at his own special time, she would talk with them about their religious life. The Wesley home in the Epworth parsonage suggests how a family life style may shape and support an individual style of life.

At ten years of age John Wesley left home for the Charterhouse School of London. There for six years and then at Oxford University for thirteen years more, both as a student and a teaching fellow, he was equipped with the best education England could give. And his mother's system and his father's love of learning went with him. His central interest, as one would expect in a young man who always maintained his sense of the continuity of life, was his consciousness of God. John Wesley always loved his old schools too, and years later he would visit them and spend a few hours in meditation. And in time Oxford recognized Wesley as one of its greatest sons:

> Wesley, John Wesley, was one of our company,
> Prophet untiring and fearless of tongue,
> Down the long years he went
> Spending yet never spent,
> Serving his God with a heart ever young.[19]

[19] Martin Schmidt, *John Wesley* (Nashville: Abingdon Press, 1962), p. 68.

It would be hard not to recognize the theme of his life.

At Oxford the Holy Club was the focus for his continually growing religious aspirations. Wesley was the leader in shaping a group of students into a fellowship of religious study, worship, and service. In his family and now in the Holy Club he worked out some of the elements which he would later use in the spiritual formation of the Methodist Society.

John Wesley's own search for God was also deeply personal. The Holy Club could not provide the answer. Neither could the Church of England, although he was ordained a deacon in 1725 and admitted to priest's orders in 1728. Nor could his mission to Georgia in 1735. In America he recognized himself as a failure. Wesley wanted desperately to find a sense of God, and thus far he could not discover any way in which to meet this hunger. He would have to participate in the shaping of a new life style which could bring him to God, and which he in turn could present to others. From this point on I will trace his intellectual and religious history as a study of this new style of life, and I will state it first in broad outline.

John Wesley was a Puritan who became a Pietist and then fused the two together into a unity of opposites. In his heritage, his upbringing and education, his discipline and conscience, he was clearly Puritan. This was the form of his asceticism. Within this experience he received the evangelical conversion of Pietism, the heartwarming experience. This was the form of the mysticism that flowed into his asceticism. His life and the Society he created are the ways in which he united Puritan dying and Pietist rising into a flowing river of experience: "So shall the sense of sinfulness you feel on the one hand and of holiness you expect on the other both contribute to establish your peace and to make it flow as a river." [20]

His Puritan Conscience

John Wesley was born into Puritanism. The English conscience had undergone a long training under Puritan preaching and Wesley's family heritage was consciously Puritan. Both his grand-

[20] John Wesley, *Forty-four Sermons* (London: Epworth Press, 1956), p. 499.

fathers suffered persecution as dissenting preachers. Samuel Wesley and then his wife, Susanna, decided on their own initiative to join the Church of England. But brought up within the Puritan parsonage, they shaped their own family life at Epworth with the self-consciousness and the God-consciousness of their heritage.

In their intensity and in their purity of heart the Wesley family was a striking picture of the Puritan home. To Samuel Wesley life was a pilgrimage, a passionate struggle in which he demonstrated great endurance. His study of the book of Job stayed with him through most of his adult life, and he finally saw it published when he was seventy-four. Susanna was as well-organized and disciplined as a Cromwell or a Milton could ever be. In her family and, when her husband was gone, in the church, she had a sense of command. She believed in breaking the self-will of her children: "When a child is corrected it must be conquered, and this will be no hard matter to do, if it be not grown headstrong by too much indulgence." [21] The system she used, however, taught self-respect as well as severity, and with her son John she achieved what she intended. He developed a stern sense of authority and a searching, self-conscious mind. Her driving passion was perfection, the perfection she saw in primitive Christianity and the Puritan perfection she saw in God. John was so thoroughly under the tutelage of his parents that this became his hope too, and across the years it was expressed in his passion for the wholeness of the Christian life—and in the endless scrupulosity of perfectionism.

The point to note, however, is that his Puritan heritage became his own before he left home and that it never left him. For a short time at Charterhouse School he reacted against the strict discipline of his home, but this was short-lived, and he reverted to the basic Puritanism of his family. Thus he was always a good and dutiful student. Away at school he set his own rules and watched over his conscience. He allowed himself five hours of sleep, he ran before breakfast, he dedicated at least one hour a day to private devotions. As soon as he was able, and through his

[21] William R. Cannon, *The Theology of John Wesley* (Nashville: Abingdon Press, 1956), p. 50.

brother Charles it became possible, he joined and then became the leader of the little Puritan colony at Oxford known as the Holy Club. Here again there is the strict spiritual formation of the intentional life. They read the classics and the Greek New Testament together. They fasted on Wednesdays and Fridays. They carried gifts to the poor and visited in the prisons. We could chart their daily schedule almost as accurately as we did for the Benedictine monks. It was the old monastic conversion of manners but out in the middle of the world. It was the highly organized Puritan way of life. In time Wesley realized that it left him hungry for a heartfelt sense of the presence of God.

His Disappointment with Mysticism

Mysticism would seem to be the answer for which John Wesley was looking, and in a way it was. He needed a deep personal experience of wonder and love to enliven his intense, introspective, Puritan mind. And so he searched the mystics and the traditional mysticism of his day for something that could give him a sense of the presence of God.

The Wesley family was deeply influenced by Roman Catholic mysticism through the reading of the mother, Susanna Wesley. This is part of her greatness, her capacity to hold together life's extremes—a disciplined will and a searching heart. Two of her favorite mystical authors were Lorenzo Scupoli and Juan de Castaniza. In them, as in her reading of Protestant mystics, she felt summoned to participate in the life of God. In his reading at Oxford three authors reintroduced Wesley to the idea of Christian perfection—Jeremy Taylor, Thomas à Kempis, and William Law. Taylor taught him the importance of the will, à Kempis convinced him of the need for a pure life, and Law inspired him to believe that perfection was possible in this life. Once he was seized by the idea of Christian perfection, it never let him go. In Georgia, and later in London, Wesley was deeply moved by two saintly Catholic mystics through two writings: *The Life of Gregory Lopez* and *The True Christian,* the life of Count Jean-Baptiste de Renty. In both these men he admired the beauty of holiness. Self-abasement was the guiding principle, and the presence of God was the goal. Taken together these books on mysticism did two things for

Wesley: they inspired him with the possibility of Christian perfection but they disappointed him with their withdrawal from the world.

Mysticism would have to come to Wesley in a form in which it would not do damage to his Puritan soul. The traditional mysticism both attracted and repelled him. He could accept dying as the goal, he could renounce the world, but neither Wesley nor Luther was willing to reject the world. And Wesley had a more vivid sense of the immanence of God and the goodness of creation. He believed that holiness and happiness go together, and for this reason he could not understand the protracted dying of mysticism. I agree with Wesley that formal mysticism tends to go too far in its dying. Yet, on the other hand, Wesley (unlike Luther) had an underdeveloped "theology of the cross." Methodism, for this reason, has never fully integrated a theology of the cross with a theology of glory. It can become overly sentimental, a little happier and a little more shallow than life allows. This euphoria, or should I say this determination to be positive, kept Wesley from fully understanding the mystics, but it also saved him from the passivity into which they can sink. So he branded the mystical life a delusion, "that poisonous mysticism," [22] and yet he still hungered for a sense of God's love in his own personal experience.

His Pietist Conversion

Mystical experience came to John Wesley through the Moravians. We might say that mysticism helped prepare him for a consciousness of God, but Puritanism played a far larger part in the creation of his basically ascetical experience. When the mystical gift came, Wesley's conversion created a new Christian style of life.

Martin Luther was a man of deep intuitive feeling, but his experience with traditional mysticism was just as unsuccessful as Wesley's. Modern man lives in the world, and he has too wide a range of experience to find peace in the art form of a cloistered life. And so despite Luther's own rich religious feeling, the Lutheran style of life looked down on those who actually set to work

[22] John Wesley, *Journal*, December 15, 1788.

and cultivated a deeply subjective religious experience. But this experience was latent in Lutheranism, and when the Romantic Age made mystical feeling respectable, mysticism came again to Germany. The Romantic movement came to the Continent before it reached England, and early in the eighteenth century German Pietism began to emphasize a practical experience of grace. It was composed of both biblical and mystical elements, and its major tenet was that we can have a deeply personal and living knowledge of Jesus Christ. The old objective sense of Lutheranism continued; it is Christ for us and not Christ in us. But now, deep within our experience, we can trust Christ alone, and we have the assurance that we trust Christ because of the new birth which will come to us through a sudden conversion experience. This is the Pietistic mysticism which Wesley was to experience.

Pietism was a broad movement within German Lutheranism. Its classical center was at Halle, but Wesley was chiefly influenced by the Moravian Pietism of Herrnhut. In 1722 a colony of Moravian refugees, descendants of the old Hussite movement of the fifteenth century in Bohemia, settled on the estate of Count Zinzendorf in Saxony. Under his inspiration and guidance the Moravian Brethren became a leaven for Pietism throughout Protestant Europe. Herrnhut became a model village. It pioneered in the development of congregational music and in its emphasis on creating a lifelong process of education. Its spirit was simple folk mysticism, a passive acceptance of Providence, even to the selecting of marriage partners through the casting of lots. The tone was sentimental and melancholy, and we read of the music almost being drowned out by the weeping at a confirmation service. Yet despite their mystical passivism the Moravians became missionaries throughout Germany and then throughout the world. They reached John Wesley on the way to Georgia, and he was immediately attracted to their definite, recognizable style of life.

In his own personal life John Wesley was at a crisis. His Puritanism had gone stale. This explains why he resigned his academic career at Oxford to become a missionary to America. The voyage lasted from November until February, and the ship nearly foundered in a storm. The mainsail split, the decks were awash with the waves, most of the passengers were in a state of panic, but the Moravians on board were singing their hymns with no sign of fear. Wesley was deeply impressed. His own personal crisis, however, deepened in Georgia: his mission to the Indians was a failure, his work among the white settlers was caught up in a factional fight, and the Sophy Hopkey affair left him disappointed in love. In this period of turmoil the Moravians seemed to offer what he needed. His association with them became constant, he searched out the meaning of their experience, and he came to see that they had a workable evangelical style of life. As the American circuit rider would have said a century later, John Wesley was on the anxious seat; he had come forward to sit on the mourner's bench. He was ready for the two-stage Methodist conversion experience. The wood had been gathered, and now the fire must fall.

On May 24, 1738, John Wesley experienced his evangelical conversion at Aldersgate. His heart, strangely enough for a Puritan, was warmed, and he had a feeling that he could trust in Christ. An assurance was given him that he had passed from death into life. It was a classical experience of dying into life: Puritan dying and Pietist rising. In one sense the experience was lifelong; in another sense it was a crisis experience through which Wesley and his converts moved. It is worth noting that the first result of this experience was an increased sense of responsibility for others. He was coming out of the depression into which he had sunk himself. A debate still continues in Methodism as to the significance of the experience at Aldersgate. Was it *the* experience or one of many? I will simply say that Aldersgate represents the time when John Wesley's Pietist feeling fused with his Puritan mind to create the Methodist style of life.

Wesley soon recognized that his new life was both like and unlike the Moravian style. He was always generous in recognizing his debt to them for his evangelical conversion. Feeling played a large role in the Methodist experience. As a matter of fact, he became more a theologian of feeling than his teachers. The Moravians believed that our experience pointed to our salvation in Christ; Wesley believed that this salvation in Christ was now experienced as Christ in us. He also differed with the Moravians on the cloistered character of their communities. They were "the still brethren"; their melancholy did not testify to the union of holiness and happiness which we are to find in the world. At this point his Puritanism asserted itself against his Pietism. He will not reject the world. The difficult thing he is trying to do is to synthesize two traditions, English Puritanism and German Pietism, into a single comprehensive style of life.

The Dying in Puritan Asceticism

The style which Wesley worked out in his own experience became the style of life for the early Methodist Society. We shall now explore its experience of Christian dying.

Through his Puritan training and his mystical reading John Wesley was thoroughly convinced of the need for a Christian dying to self. In Jeremy Taylor's devotional guide, *The Rule and Exercises of Holy Dying,* he was familiar with the old "art of dying," but Wesley was closer to the Puritan mind. "Repentance" and "self-denial" were the words he used in his preaching. "First, repent; that is, know yourself. . . . Know yourself to be a sinner. . . . Know that you are corrupted." [23] And how do we know this? Is it a gift that comes only to the elect? Here Wesley broke with Puritanism. The common grace of God teaches everyone to recognize sin and to know the need of repentance. And we are to know this, not as a degenerating despair, not with the "fierce, sour, and bitter spirit" [24] of Scotland's John Knox, but in a direct and rational way which should lead us immediately to God's grace.

Wesley worked out ways of convincing men and women that they should accept the truth of repentance and self-denial. In one way or another he preached dying to self in every sermon: "Men must be wounded before they go in trustful search of the Physician who alone can heal." [25] And his sermons, unlike those of a great and enthusiastic preacher like George Whitefield, were directed to the single solitary individual. He preached for a conviction of sin. This experience of dying was also written into the Wesleyan hymns, and his followers were led into an ascetical self-examination while they sang: "I want a sober mind, a self-renouncing will . . . . I want a godly fear, a quick discerning

[23] Wesley, *Forty-four Sermons,* p. 79.

[24] Francis Gerald Ensley, *John Wesley, Evangelist* (Nashville: Tidings, 1955), p. 30.

[25] *Ibid.,* p. 27.

eye." [26] All this is Puritan with its obsession with individuality, but with a direct, sober-minded way of bringing the individual into a confrontation with God.

Wesley then proceeded to build this ascetical dying into a life-long experience of self-denial. In a sermon on "Self-Denial" he preached a theology of the cross: "The *denying* ourselves, and the *taking up our cross* . . . is absolutely, indispensably necessary, either to our becoming or continuing his disciples." [27] His acute consciousness of time, I think, was his greatest ascetical discipline, but there was virtually nothing that he did not organize in his own life, and he made the rules for himself. He cast his movement in his own image. Thus at his annual conferences, he reminded his ministers to rise at four in the morning and to sleep just six hours a night. He had rules against the wearing of ribbons and the drinking of tea. He disapproved of pleasantries of speech and lively wits. Of course, he also had rules for which we would have more sympathy, rules against smuggling, drunkenness, and all the petty sins of our personal lives. In one form or another he was always the scrupulous Puritan watching over himself and examining his followers. Maybe the worst picture we can paint is of Wesley parading the children of Kingswood through the morgue to teach them that life always stands in danger of death. This, of course, is an eighteenth-century view of life that is especially shocking to us. Some of these severe restraints and disciplines were moderated in Wesley's later life, but his basic asceticism remained. His followers had such a great joy in life that it is surprising and sobering to recognize the Puritan self-denial which underlay the Methodist experience.

John Wesley's deepest experience of Christian dying was apparently known only to his brother Charles. When he confessed the whole truth, as he did in a letter which he wrote to his brother Charles at the age of sixty-three, he could say, "I do not love God, I never did." [28] We are to take this not as the confession of

[26] Charles Wesley, "Jesus, My Strength, My Hope," from the second and third stanzas.

[27] Wesley, *Forty-four Sermons,* pp. 554-55.

[28] *The Letters of the Rev. John Wesley* (London: Epworth Press, 1931), V, 16.

a pagan but as that of an honest Puritan in whom dying, at least for the moment, is dominant.

Sometimes the negative is surprisingly positive. It is hard to tell. The Puritan mind, as we noted earlier, "repented of its repentance." That is, it feared that even our repentance can be motivated by selfish reasons. On one level this is a negative despair, but on another level it is a positive humility. Wesley's confession of unbelief (not disbelief) was an experinece of despair and dying, but it was also undertaken before God. Sometimes, strangely enough, dying is not just a "preparation" for life, but the denial and dying is in some sense a positive virtue which shares in the gift of life. Our confession of sin is also a recognition of grace. I wish Wesley, like Augustine and Luther, could have made this confession more often and more publicly. But the major point to make is that Wesley was honest with himself in recognizing Christian dying, not just in his beliefs and in his preaching, not just in the Methodist style of life, but at the center of his existence. The great virtue that followed, and that has always to some extent characterized the Methodist experience, was happiness, holiness, and joy.

The Rising in Pietist Mysticism

The goal of the Methodist experience was "life in God," and Moravian Pietism made it possible. Puritan dying was now followed by Pietist rising. The discipline which Wesley undertook as a Puritan was thorough, but it was not arranged in a series of stages. His Pietism, however, was a progressive experience, and a member of the Methodist Society could locate where he stood on the road to salvation.

Three great theological words describe the basic steps in the Methodist experience. Wesley used the images of a porch, a door, and a house. The porch was repentance, the door was faith, and the house was holiness. Repentance, we have already noted, was spelled out in his Puritanism. That was the porch and it came first. Next came the door of faith through which we are justified. Ever since the apostle Paul we have asked for more than Jesus' simple trust; we have needed an assurance that we do trust in God. Now, through the Moravian internalization of Luther's ethic of grace, Wesley believed that we could actually experience our own justification. It is the gift of God's grace, and it is the full, free, present assurance that God accepts us. In it God removes our guilt, takes away the power of sin, and gives us a new birth. All of these things can happen simultaneously, but the early Methodists also viewed them as a series of consecutive stages in the experience of salvation. At a particular time, probably as an answer to a personal crisis, a heartwarming experience would break in upon the serious seeker. It meant that he had entered the house of holiness and that he had received his own justification by faith.

The house of the religious life was holiness, and this was the major emphasis in the Methodist experience. It was known by a number of names: sanctification, entire sanctification, holiness, scriptural holiness, love, perfect love, or perfection. We are to be "justified by faith and perfected in love." [29] These two steps would usually come at the same time, but two different things are taking place. Whereas justification places its emphasis on what God has done for us, sanctification stresses what we, under the guidance of the Spirit, can do to approach God. This experience of holiness, or sanctification, is the progressive growth of the Christian life, and it can culminate in perfection. Every Christian must cross the porch of repentance, enter the door of justification by faith, and live in the house of holiness. Then, as a Christian, he will want to serve God in holiness and "go on to perfection."

Wesley had a great deal of trouble with the word "perfection." It was not, he said, an absolute and infallible perfection; it was not sinless; it involved growth. The believer is not perfect in knowledge, and he is not above making mistakes or falling into temptation. These disclaimers helped. His definition of what it was, however, was not entirely successful. Perfection, he wrote, is simply love. It is the fulfillment of Jesus' great commandment on love; it is the triumph of God's love in the human will. The question is whether there is a state in the Christian life where God's love is actually fulfilled in something that could be called perfection.

In his doctrine of perfection John Wesley was wrestling with the ultimate goal in the Christian life. What should it be, and can it be attained? Each Christian life style must define its final ob-

[29] Cannon, *The Theology of John Wesley*, p. 7.

jective because that sets the direction in which to go. Wesley's goal of perfection was a synthesis of at least two elements in his experience. One was the heartwarming experience at Aldersgate, and the other was the training in holiness that began in his home at Epworth. These two elements were his Pietism and his Puritanism. Or, from a slightly different perspective, the two elements were his justification by faith (what God does for us) and his sanctification (what we, in the Spirit, do for God). G. C. Cell describes the two as "an original and unique synthesis of the Protestant ethic of grace with the Catholic ethic of holiness." [30] Perfection was a gift of God, and yet it was also dynamically growing and changing. It brought together and held together the polarities in Wesley's experience.

John Wesley believed that the state of perfection was made possible by God's divine immanence. "God worketh in you; therefore, you can work." [31] God works through our shining moments and our ongoing processes. He blesses us in Pietism and in our Puritanism (or, if you prefer, our Anglican "Catholicism"). God works in both. In the state of perfection, Wesley had created an experience something like Benedict's "peace of God" and John of the Cross's "union with God." All three believed in an achievable perfection. All three believed that our resurrection rising can finally carry us, at least in some very definite present way, beyond the dying *and* rising of Pauline Christianity.

Wesleyan perfection, like Benedict's peace and John of the Cross's union, was premature. There is no state of perfection in this life.[32] The apostle Paul is the great interpreter of the Christian experience: "We have died, and we *will* rise." We must always stay within the tension of Christian dying and rising. Even Paul did not fully understand the guidelines which he had established. The early church had little understanding of spiritual sins, and it never occurred to Paul that a man Christ had won could be conquered again by evil. Luther was needed to deepen Paul's original insight. We might now say: "We *are* dying, and we *are* ris-

[30] Cell, *The Rediscovery of John Wesley* (New York: Henry Holt and Co., 1935), p. 347.

[31] Cannon, *The Theology of John Wesley*, p. 100.

[32] John Wesley's definition of sin was inadequate. He defined it as a *thing* that can be removed like cancer, rather than as a *tendency* with which we must continue to wrestle.

ing." Wesley, like Benedict and John of the Cross, did not fully maintain the "eschatological reservation."

But John Wesley, perhaps better than Benedict or John of the Cross, understood the limits of dying and rising in his own life. He knew that *he* did not live in a state of perfection. And, except for a few of his followers, he expected it to come to most Christians at the moment of death. That, of course, is the only time when our "trouble, sorrow, suffering, and death are forever past." [33] A "state" of perfection in this life is not possible, but in creating the "direction" of perfection Wesley was apostolic. A few of the early Methodists believed that they had received a "second blessing," the experience of perfection within the house of holiness. Now they could consciously and willingly do no wrong. We must believe they were in error; in our psychological understanding of life no one is perfected and pure. I do not know whether they were mainly a help or a hindrance. Their self-righteousness could have been unbearable, but their self-sacrificing zeal might also have led a church forward in love. They were to be perfect in love. But most of the early Methodists did not claim to be perfect. For them the goal of perfection was a powerful incentive and an apostolic direction. In struggling to "go on to perfection" they led beautiful apostolic lives of dying and rising with Christ.

The Methodist experience—despite the theological words with which it can be described—had a deeply moving, heartfelt appeal. The poor, especially the talented poor who still had some hope for release, found it a genuine way of achieving self-acceptance and then self-expression. They felt the experience, and they learned the theological words which described what they felt—the new birth, assurance, holiness, and perfection. Field preaching was probably their first contact with the Methodists. There Wesley, or perhaps one of his lay preachers, would preach to create a conversion crisis. Godly sorrow and creative despair were to motivate a desire for belief. Those to whom the message appealed were organized into classes, bands, and what we might call seminars in holiness. This was Wesley's adaptation of the Moravian emphasis on education. New services were added to

---

[33] The funeral liturgy of the Church of England.

the preaching service to deepen the intensity of the experience. Here we have the yearly covenant service, the monthly watch night services, and the frequent love feasts. To these were added the regular services of the Church of England, and Wesley himself received Communion on an average of once every four to five days throughout his long ministry.[34] The Benedictine monastery structured an outward form of life, and Carmelite mysticism created a deeply interior pattern. The Methodist style was both outward and inward, but not as an experience for an elite, and not cloistered from the world. John Wesley had two great gifts which he wrote into the Methodist style of life: a consciousness of God and "a talent for practical administration amounting to genius." [35]

Joy and happiness were the crowning experiences of Methodist rising with Christ. "Every believer," Wesley wrote, "ought to enjoy life." [36] In Wesley himself this was only partly realized. He was so busy, preaching fifteen times a week, traveling five thousand miles a year, and superintending at the end the seventy thousand souls in his movement in England. Puritan discipline kept a heavy hand on his Pietist joy. Among his followers, however, the weight of Puritanism was never so heavy, and it was gradually lifted. The hymns of the early Methodists carry the rapturous joy of their resurrection rising:

> Fully justified I,
> I rode in the sky
>   Nor envied Elijah his seat.
> In a chariot of fire
> My soul mounted higher,
>   And the moon, it was under my feet.[37]

And this joy was not just a private experience. It was "in Christ." The sixty-five hundred hymns of Charles Wesley are Christ-centered with Jesus as a "verbal crucifix" [38] and then, as promised and proven in the Methodist experience, as a real presence.

---

[34] J. Ernest Rattenbury, *The Eucharistic Hymns of John and Charles Wesley* (London: Epworth Press, 1948), pp. 7-8.

[35] Francis J. McConnell, *John Wesley* (Nashville: Abingdon Press, 1939), p. 9.

[36] Ensley, *John Wesley, Evangelist*, p. 31.

[37] McConnell, *John Wesley*, p. 95.

[38] Rattenbury, *The Eucharistic Hymns of John and Charles Wesley*, p. 22.

The kingdom of God had begun to come, not just for them, but in them. And the joy of Christ's presence was shared. "The flame of love ran from heart to heart," Wesley wrote of a meeting, "and scarcely any remained unmoved." [39] The Wesleyan movement in its more than fifty sects produced the perfectionists and pentecostals of American history, and like the Jewish Hasidim and the Catholic Franciscans they came to represent the enthusiasts with the heartwarming experience.

The Methodist Life Style in John Wesley

How well did Wesley succeed? How well did early Methodism reinterpret the theme of dying into life? We know very little of the personal lives of Paul, Benedict, and John of the Cross, but Wesley was a public figure and he lived relatively recently. I find myself in accord with traditional interpretation of his life. We can be critical of his experience, but sympathetic of his very great achievement.

We might begin with where he failed and the way in which he failed. John Wesley, I believe, was an uneven balance of the Puritan will and Pietist sentiment. He was always more Puritan than Pietist. All his biographers agree that he was an autocrat in his Society. He was not a warm person, and he was far too independent to tie himself down to anyone. His life is marked with a long line of broken friendships; he broke with nearly everyone he could not control—the Moravians, Count Zinzendorf, William Law, George Whitefield, Thomas Maxfield (his first lay preacher), and his wife.[40] He was so highly organized that he was never at leisure. He drilled his people hard. He was a lonely person. He was always the Puritan disciplinarian.

His feeling, as a Pietist or simply as a human being, was never allowed to achieve a full range of expression. He spoke of feeling, he preached a heartwarming experience, but he seldom revealed himself in depth, except for his "spiritual feelings." Part of what I am saying is a criticism of the culture of his day. Thus the Romantic movement at last made it possible to appreciate nature, and Wesley was one of the first to admire a beautiful land-

[39] Ensley, *John Wesley, Evangelist,* p. 29.
[40] McConnell, *John Wesley,* p. 323.

scape. There his feelings were open. But he scorned the British Museum, he saw no reason why children should ever play, and he believed that the world was fit to be consumed on the Last Day. This was the restriction laid upon him by eighteenth-century culture and religion. But in his own personal life, as in his marriage, he failed to show a gentle grace. A few days after the marriage he began to preach on celibacy, and he wrote to his wife that she was to be "ruled by her husband as he was ruled by Christ." [41] Except for his sisters, whom he could help, he proved a poor intimate. And yet he gave virtually all his money away, he worked almost every waking hour for what he considered to be the cause of Christ, and in the last letter which he wrote, he commended William Wilberforce in his work in Parliament against "that execrable villainy, which is the scandal of religion . . . American slavery." [42] A strange irony. He was not intimate, and yet his whole life was an act of self-giving.

The Wesleyan style of life, if I may turn to its positive contribution, was endlessly open and sharply defined. In its openness it was a synthesis of many of the great archetypes of Christian history—the apostle, monk, mystic, reformer, Puritan, and Pietist. The Methodist style was comprehensive, and Wesley was able to develop an "outwardness" and an "inwardness" and a life in the world. In his Society he would gather a seminar to study the good that God is doing in other Christians. In all this, Methodism was not a revolt against the church, but an attempt to recover the full Christian life. Yet at the same time Methodism centered down on an intense experience, what Bonhoeffer called a "secret discipline." Wesley was not Paul, the genius who is always open to a wide range of experience. Wesley cultivated a specific style, one which was a fusion of the two great traditions in American Protestant history: Puritanism and Pietism. With Puritan activism and Moravian quietism he shaped a new form of dying and rising with Christ. As a style it was sharply defined to meet the religious crisis of the eighteenth century, and yet it was also faithful to the historic passion for Christian wholeness. Most amazing of all, the Methodist way of life was carried to common, ordinary people. It was as if John Wesley had recreated the

[41] *Ibid.*, p. 227.
[42] *The Letters of the Rev. John Wesley*, VIII, 265.

outward discipline of the Benedictine monastic school and the inward progression of the Carmelite mystical experience in the apostolic arena where Paul wrestled with life in the world. All men of goodwill can be proud of his achievement.

But the Wesleyan synthesis did not last; it never does. No form is final. Puritan dying was crowded out by an aggressive, overly simplified Pietism. The two-stage conversion experience was lost. In early Methodism the conviction of sin came first. The seeker might come forward to sit on the mourners' bench, and he would wait for the witness of the Spirit. By 1850 you could decide to become a Christian without waiting for the Spirit. You would come forward to the altar rail or, at a still later time, raise your hand in the pew. The old Puritan discipline was lost, and the old Pietist "gifts and graces" were going. In its openness Methodism found itself open to a world that had gone secular.

John Wesley was Sören Kierkegaard's "knight of infinity" in eighteenth-century England. Perfection, if it is conceived poetically and spiritually, is a beautiful word. It is Paul's word too. For Kierkegaard the Christian's goal is to express the infinite in the finite, "to transform life's leap into a walk." [43] John Wesley's life, 1703-1791, was a very long walk, single-file in the early days while he and his brother Charles read to each other on the way, and then later John alone, in a life of dying and rising, on the roads of England.

[43] Walter Lowrie, *Kierkegaard* (New York: Oxford University Press, 1938), p. 270.

5 ❧ The Classical Dimensions of the American Dream

An antagonism may naturally arise between the healthy-minded way of viewing life and the way that takes all this experience of evil as something essential. . . . It seems to me that we are bound to say that morbid-mindedness ranges over the wider scale of experience, and that its survey is the one that overlaps. The method of averting one's attention from evil, and living simply in the light of good is splendid as long as it will work. It will work with many persons; it will work far more generally than most of us suppose; and within the sphere of its successful operation there is nothing to be said against it as a religious solution. But it breaks down impotently as soon as melancholy comes; and even though one be quite free from melancholy one's self, there is no doubt that healthy-mindedness is inadequate as a philosophical doctrine, because evil facts which it refuses positively to account for are a genuine portion of reality; and they may after all be the best key to life's significance. . . . In their extreme forms . . . you all recognize the difference: you understand, for example, the disdain of the methodist convert for the mere skyblue healthy-minded moralist; and you likewise enter into the aversion of the latter to what seems to him the diseased subjectivism of the Methodist, dying to live, as he calls it, and making of paradox and the inversion of natural appearances the essence of God's truth.

William James, *The Varieties of Religious Experience*[1]

The healthy-minded begin with life, the twice-born begin with dying; but both, especially the twice-born but even the once-born, must die into life. In this fifth chapter we shall explore two complementary life styles—the lives of Walt Whitman and Herman Melville—as expressions of the dying into life in the American Dream.

[1] (New York: New American Library, 1958), pp. 137-41.

111

The Puritan Becomes a Yankee

We are what we are because of a long history of spiritual formation, and what may seem to be our own individual styles of life may be largely our choice of a stock character which history made possible at a particular time. Our life styles are simply our expression of this character in our daily living. "We think in generalizations," Whitehead wrote, "but we live in detail." [2] Let me trace the way in which the Puritan became a Yankee.

Three major movements helped define the character of the Yankee—Puritanism in the seventeenth century, the Age of Reason in the eighteenth century, and the Romantic movement in the nineteenth century until the Civil War. In England, John Wesley was able to synthesize something of all three into a single style of life. He was an ascetic Puritan, a man of reason, and a Pietist with a heartwarming experience. In Colonial America, Jonathan Edwards, the Puritan preacher who inspired the Great Awakening, sought essentially the same synthesis. But here on a new continent there was less continuity and more radical change. Each of these movements contributed something to the shaping of the Yankee.

First, the old Puritan theology with its original sin and its unforgiving God bcame unbelievable, and in 1805 the Unitarians captured Harvard College. Puritan thought was transformed into transcendentalism, and in this form, which we shall examine in a few pages, we can trace its continuing influence. In the Age of Reason, secondly, we can also note what was left behind and what was carried forward in the formation of the Yankee. The dominant role assigned to reason now gave way to an emotional sensibility, and the social ideals of an ordered society were transformed to fit the "innocent situation" of the American frontier. Something was lost, but the natural rights of the Age of Reason— life, liberty, and the pursuit of happiness—were taken up in the individualism, the pragmatism, and the naturalism of the new Romantic movement. By the nineteenth century a great deal had changed. Romanticism rejected the Puritan doctrine of man's natural depravity, and it worshiped a new ideal of man's natural

[2] Whitehead, *Science and Philosophy,* p. 36.

goodness. By the middle of the century the new style of life that emerged was transcendental, individualistic, and emotional. These broad generalizations fit the character of the Yankee, the life style that was to dominate America in the nineteenth century.

In the Yankee, religion continued to play an active role. The church was transformed and secularized and carried forward into the new age. Faith became intensely personal and individual; an itinerant preacher was thought to be qualified to define the sin in any man's heart. American Pietism, now free from the theology and asceticism of the Puritan, became the natural folk mysticism of the Romantic movement; and all along the frontier it inspired a pentecostal revivalism from the turn of the century to the Civil War. Through preaching a crisis was created, an experience was expected, and then with a changed heart the new convert would go right back into his life on the farm. Religion was becoming increasingly secularized, and secular life was not separate from the influence of religion. We shall see later the very important role religion unconsciously played in the thinking of Walt Whitman and Herman Melville.

Yankee society, despite the sweeping generalizations with which I have described it, was surprisingly provincial. We began with an Old World sophistication, but on the frontier as it retreated westward we became young and naïve. At first, on winning our independence from Britain, the old colonial ways hung on for decades. Although the government in Washington coined money in quarter dollars, people during the War of 1812 still referred to these coins as two shillings. America was a provincial culture that only very gradually recognized its own independent destiny, and not until the Civil War did it realize that it was to become a continental empire. We were a series of provinces with weak ties. In New England, as in the South, there were those like Nathaniel Hawthorne, who welcomed the Civil War as an opportunity for his region to gain its independence.

A number of forces, however, were working to change the integrity of the tidewater republic. The population explosion would be one; New York City with two hundred thousand people in 1835 absorbed one million by 1860. A second force for change was the coming of science and industry. At first the farmers disliked anything that tampered with their traditional way of working with the soil. By 1845 this had changed, and a lecturer could imagine that the hiss of the serpent and the scream of the wild bird "would be far less pleasant to the senses than the hum of industry, or the noise of traffic." [3] The third and overwhelming force for change was the war itself, and now in a short time provincial America became a continental empire. With the war and with the growth of industry we would take the route of the commercial republic, a perhaps unavoidable venture thus far of over one hundred years. It has brought many regrets, but we may have had no other way to go. But then, in the mid-nineteenth century and at the height of the two-hundred-and-fifty-year-old provincial culture, there was a literary flowering and a search for a fresh vision of the American dream.

Our Greatest Poet and Our Greatest Novelist

Moby Dick was published in 1851 and *Leaves of Grass* in 1855. Herman Melville and Walt Whitman are now generally recognized as two of the greatest imaginative writers in American literary history. Both wrote a new prose poetry: Whitman in the blank verse that lies between lyrical poetry and prose, and Melville in the form of a romance with a chase sequence in *Moby Dick,* which is the most dramatic epic in our literature. I agree with the judgment that the English poets take precedence over the American;[4] we have no equal to Shakespeare, Milton, Donne, Keats, Hopkins, or Yeats. Our artists have, until recently, lacked the spiritual richness of the original English-speaking culture. But taken together, Walt Whitman and Herman Melville present the full range of the American vision, "land and sea, day and night, sunlight and shadow, triumph and tragedy." [5] For our purposes their poetic epics are complementary interpretations of life and death in the American Dream.

Through strange coincidence these two men shared a common background. Both were born in New York in 1819; both spent

---

[3] Perry Miller, *The Life of the Mind in America* (New York: Harcourt, Brace, and World, 1965), p. 301.

[4] Chase, *Emily Dickinson,* p. 254.

[5] Lewis Mumford, *Herman Melville* (New York: Harcourt, Brace, and Co., 1929), p. 367.

most of their lives in or near that city; both died at the age of seventy-two; but they never met. The significant thing they had in common was the transcendentalist vision of life. In the American culture, especially as interpreted in our literature, we have always placed our major emphasis on either the very specific or the idealistic and abstract. Our literature has shown little concern for the intermediate range of institutions in between, such as the family, the school, the church, business, or the community. Thus we have been preoccupied with the individual: the Puritans with their eternal soul and now the Transcendentalists with their god-like self. Without this emphasis on local institutions, as with the extended family circle in Russian literature, the self is seen against the great reality and generality of the nation, a nation that is emergent, democratic, idealistic, progressive, and perfectible. The goal of life for the Transcendentalist was to create a primitive Eden, at once behind us on the frontier and ahead of us in the future as a paradise on earth for both the individual and the nation. These beliefs were axiomatic for Walt Whitman and Herman Melville; but with their differing temperaments, one an optimist and the other a pessimist, the personal shaping of their common inheritance was radically different.

In *The Varieties of Religious Experience,* William James set forward a useful way of interpreting these two approaches to life. From Francis W. Newman he borrowed a description of two types of religious experience: "God has two families of children on this earth, the once-born and the twice-born." [6] The first are the healthy-minded with their vision of natural goodness, and the second are the twice-born with their essentially tragic sense of life. William James named Walt Whitman "the supreme contemporary example" [7] of the first, and we might describe Herman Melville as a classic illustration of the second. Whitman begins with a joyful acceptance of life, and he seems to reject what we have called Christian dying. Melville, on the other hand, begins with an acceptance of the tragedy in life, but he then works to bring "the whole soul of man into activity." [8] Both the once-born

[6] James, *The Varieties of Religious Experience,* pp. 77-78.
[7] *Ibid.,* p. 80.
[8] Francis O. Matthiessen, *American Renaissance* (New York: Oxford University Press, 1941), p. 656.

115

and the twice-born can help illuminate the theme of Christian dying in the modern world. They demonstrate that this process is universal, it touches everyone, and that it takes place in the secular as well as in the sacred. The way in which Americans approach the themes of life and death is central to understanding our national style of life.

A Vision of Life's Natural Goodness

Walt Whitman was almost unique among creative artists in having the lifelong support of a loving and devoted family. Born May 31, 1819, of Puritan and English stock through his father, Quaker and Dutch through his mother, he came from a good family, farming folk on an excellent Long Island farm inherited from more successful ancestors. It was a happy home in which he was devoted to his mother, and she, in turn, throughout her life loved him as a son who could do no wrong. There was suffering too. The family fortunes declined, there were two defectives in the family—in later years in Camden he slept in the same bed with his imbecile brother Eddie—and in his old age Walt was hurt to the heart with his own failure. But the family love never failed. At the deaths of his mother, his sister Martha, and his two grandmothers, he spoke of them as "the best and sweetest women I ever saw, or ever expect to see." [9] He went forth from the family, as he wrote, with a "yearning and swelling heart." [10]

To this natural love of life add the vigor and enthusiasm of the best years this nation will ever know, and you have a healthy, outgoing, bearded young man, "an American, one of the roughs, a Kosmos," [11] as he said of himself. In him, Van Wyck Brooks believed, the national character "precipitated" and a synthesis of our native spirituality was achieved.[12] Walt was successively printer, newspaperman, schoolteacher, male nurse, sage, and above all poet. He needed no wife, not because of any homosexual

[9] Henry Seidel Canby, *Walt Whitman* (Boston: Houghton Mifflin, 1943), p. 11.

[10] Richard Chase, *Walt Whitman Reconsidered* (New York: William Sloane, 1955), p. 26.

[11] Walt Whitman, *Complete Poetry and Selected Prose* (Boston: Houghton Mifflin, 1959), p. 41.

[12] Chase, *Walt Whitman Reconsidered*, p. 16.

tendency, but because for him the world was a wedding. He was in love with himself; he loved to declaim his poems in the open air in an outpouring of emotion, but he was saved from an isolating egotism by his fellow-feeling. Newspaper work meant free entrance to the theater, the plays and the operas; and for him life was to be seen and savored and sung. In 1860 he said that "but for the opera I could never have written *Leaves of Grass.*" [13] Poetry, of course, was his life, the evocation of life that enlarged his world, a world which he presented to America in 1855 for what he hoped would be, as Emerson named it, "the American Poem."

The romantic and mystical optimism that fused his life with the world was Quaker, surprisingly Quaker when we note their customs and his character. His mother's family was Quaker, and sixty years later he could remember his father saying of Elias Hicks, the leader of the mystical revival in the Society of Friends, "Come, mother, Elias preaches tonight." [14] Walt called the months by their Quaker names, "first month, second month, third . . ." He wore his hat like a Quaker, indoors and out. He was called "The Good Gray Poet"; the color of cloth he wore was Quaker gray. In temperament he was either all activity or quietistic in his withdrawal from life. Again, Quaker. A mystic inwardness and a mutual helpfulness, the two features of the Friends, describe him too. He could not kill, he once said during the Civil War, because he was "Quaker." [15] In Whitman's last years Elias Hicks's portrait hung in his room, and he wrote an essay three years before his death in defense of the Quaker leader to show that the source of theology is "in yourself." [16] Walt Whitman always had faith in Quaker intuition, a secular Quaker faith outside the meeting house, but not outside the love of God. In one of his last poems he wrote, "Old, poor, and paralyzed, I thank Thee." [17]

But it was a life without a conscious sense of limits, an effusive yes without a restraining no. Whitman had what Henry Seidel Canby describes as "negative capability," the capacity to fuse a world of experience but without a core into which the experience is assimilated. "He is more like a funnel for the sensations and

[13] Matthiessen, *American Renaissance*, pp. 559-60.
[14] *Ibid.*, p. 538. [15] *Ibid.*, p. 537. [16] *Ibid.*, p. 538.
[17] *Complete Poetry and Selected Prose*, p. 296. Whitman is speaking for himself in this "Prayer of Columbus."

the wandering ideas of this world. They flow in, they flow out, channelled toward democracy, made articulate by his style." [18] At its best it is all life; at its worst it does not know how to deal with death. As death came upon Whitman throughout his life, he could only suffer and die a little. He had no way of turning dying into life.

And Walt Whitman had so much dying in his life. *Leaves of Grass* sold only twelve copies. It was a terrible blow. The Civil War saved him; it gave him a new direction. He became a self-annihilating visitor to perhaps one hundred thousand sick and wounded soldiers. Soon after the war he was struck down half-paralyzed; with this and, as the autopsy showed later, a number of other painful illnesses, he suffered for nineteen years until his death. In this period he lived with his brother George. He won a small band of followers, he gave a few lectures, but his poetic fire died down, and he spent his days revising his letter to America. He still had what he called "Good Moments," but as he grew older he became effusive and bland, never knowing how to take the dying that came upon him, the death that can wound the well-being of even the healthy-minded. In the details of living he was canny and prudential, but in his overall strategy he did not know how to deal with the over-againstness of life. He never outgrew his adolescent optimism.

We must see Walt Whitman on a number of different levels; he said of himself, "I am large, I contain multitudes." [19] He was a gregarious, happy man; children loved him, the soldiers cheered him. But he was also lonely: an alienated artist with no friends. He loved himself, but he doubted himself too. There is more than self-pity in his beautiful poem, "As I Ebb'd with the Ocean of Life." He was a failure in the world, but it was a hostile world to a poet. I would like to judge his life, however, not at its worst in the paralysis of his old age, but when he was at his best in his poetry, creating a vision of natural goodness.

The Life in "Leaves of Grass"

Life, not life out of death, nor life and death, but life and more life, is the theme of *Leaves of Grass*. The life is the vitality

[18] Canby, *Walt Whitman*, pp. 353-54. [19] *Ibid.*, p. 284.

of the American Dream, the idealized life of the New World. Life, like grass, has the individuality of a single spear of grass—the individual hero; and life is also our common life as a field of grass —the brotherhood of man, the comrades of the open road. Walt Whitman intended his poem to be the American epic, "a programme of chants" for "Americanos," [20] to evoke the heroic qualities of life and more life for the whole of mankind.

The central paradox is the tension between the self and the all of life everywhere, the simple separate person and the "Enmasse." [21] Beginning with himself Whitman expands life into greater and greater diversity until he includes all that we are, body and soul, and all men everywhere in the dream of "the Nation of many nations." [22] The opposites in his poems merge on many levels, individualistic, democratic, and mystical. As an individual he enlarges life to include the whole body—sex and its claim upon us. He is, as he wrote down in his notebook, "the poet of the body." [23] Greatness is growth, and American democracy is to be inclusive of the Southerner and the Northerner, the Kentuckian and the Californian: "Of every hue and caste am I, of every rank and religion." [24] He loved the countryside, but he was chiefly a city man, and more than any other poet he "made the city available to literature." [25] Science and industry and politics carry his dream along. Out of his experience as a journalist he developed an eye for the flow of life, the body and the soul, and the masses of the new age on the open road.

The keynote of this new life is love: "A kelson [keel] of the creation is love," [26] It will call all life together, and it will not destroy our individuality. God is the final comrade at the end of the road. He is also the Great *Camarado* along life's journey; and we are now "walking the old hills of Judaea with the beautiful gentle God by my side." [27] Walt Whitman's aim in fusing all of life together is not to reduce us to animals, but to lift us to the life of the spirit.

[20] James E. Miller, Jr., *A Critical Guide to Leaves of Grass* (Chicago: University of Chicago Press, 1966), p. 258.

[21] *Complete Poetry and Selected Prose*, p. 40.

[22] *Ibid.*, p. 36.   [23] *Ibid.*, p. 39.   [24] *Ibid.*, p. 36.

[25] Miller, *A Critical Guide to Leaves of Grass*, p. 61.

[26] Matthiessen, *American Renaissance*, p. 546.

[27] *Complete Poetry and Selected Prose*, p. 50.

Rising with Walt Whitman

Walt Whitman's poetry is a secular interpretation of Christian rising into life. The self is divine—both the Quakers and the Transcendentalists taught him this—and the world is also divine. Life is a reaching out of the self for a new consciousness as it merges and fuses with the world. The physical, the social, and the spiritual are to be synthesized into a new democratic self. This is a secular version of Paul's coming kingdom, Benedict's peace of God, John of the Cross's union with God, and Wesley's perfection in love. To Walt Whitman resurrection rising lies in our human perfectibility, and the self in perfect freedom is the "eligible" heir of everything in life.

Where are we to find this perfection? It is found in what is natural—not the natural that is primitive, but the natural in civilization. Artificiality must be stripped away, and we must return to the simple things. Whitman practiced this perfection in his own life. On the hospital wards in Washington,

> Behold, I do not give lectures or a little charity,
> When I give I give myself.[28]

This perfection was the goal of his imagination wherever there was suffering:

> I am the man, I suffer'd, I was there.[29]

This perfection can be everywhere because it lies as a real reality beneath everything that is: nature, the city, sex, even whatever we might choose to call bad. "What is called good is perfect and what is called bad is just as perfect." [30] At this point Whitman was beginning to look for a truth deeper than surface appearance. We all do this, and Whitman did it in his peculiarly Quaker way of retreating periodically from the pressures of life to regain his sense of balance in the woods and fields of Long Island. But he was also doing more than this, and the question is whether he achieved a genuinely mystical way of rising into life.

[28] Canby, *Walt Whitman*, p. 227.
[29] *Complete Poetry and Selected Prose*, p. 51.
[30] James, *The Varieties of Religious Experience*, p. 86.

James E. Miller develops the very interesting thesis that the "Song of Myself" is a dramatic description of the mystical experience.[31] The central portion of the poem, he believes, can "be related, step by step, to the 'Mystic Way' as described by Evelyn Underhill." [32] These stages are named as the awakening of the self, the purification of the self, illumination, the dark night of the soul, and union with God. The difference between Whitman and the orthodox Christian mystic is that growth is achieved, not by the mortification of the senses, but through their transfiguration: "The senses are not humbled but glorified." [33] It is a rising, but not a dying and rising, into life.

A similar mystical experience is found in Harvey Cox's belief that a sensory overload achieves much the same result as sensory deprivation.[34] Formerly, he writes, the ascetic tried to free his consciousness by minimizing his sensory inputs through silence, plain clothes, meager food; but now we can achieve the same thing through pounding the senses with so many inputs that they cannot cope with the pressure. Cox apparently believes that this will drive us into the dark night of the soul where we might be open to God. In this way the new overloading of the senses, this multimedia blow-out, might achieve much the same thing as the old austerities. It would call for an inversion of the mystical experience, one peculiarly suited to the healthy-minded. It is a divinization of man. I believe, however, that without self-denial and asceticism to humble a man, this healthy-minded mysticism can become utterly selfish. It does not know the limits of the self because self-consciousness must be learned through suffering and an act of collision. The mystical experience, without denial and dying, can easily become demoralized or demonic.

I think James Miller is correct in recognizing the mystical unity in Walt Whitman, but incomplete in his suggestion that it is similar to the orthodox Christian mysticism in Evelyn Underhill's writings. Yet Whitman's goal, though not his way to the goal, was shaped by the Christian faith. He is reaching for an imaginative union with God, and the twelve poems in *Leaves of Grass* are also

---

[31] Miller, *A Critical Guide to Leaves of Grass,* p. 6.
[32] *Ibid.,* p. 7. [33] *Ibid.,* p. 10.
[34] Cox, *The Feast of Fools* (Cambridge: Harvard University Press, 1969), pp. 108-10.

apparently arranged to demonstrate the progression of this mystical evolution. He "penetrates through the material world into the spiritual," [35] and he invokes God's blessing on his work: "Bathe me O God in thee." [36] The question is not whether it is mystical, but what kind of mysticism are we to recognize in his cosmic consciousness.

I believe that it is helpful to see levels of mysticism in Walt Whitman's poetry. First there is the resurrection rising of the body, the spiritualization of the material, the divinization of all that we are. In personal terms this is similar to the inner light of the Quakers; in cosmic terms it is similar to the Greek Orthodox belief that all creation is sanctified with the presence of God. It is similar in its goals, but Walt Whitman is shaping a basically different approach. The new consciousness also raises us above reality, above all the limitations of life, into an Eden-like innocence where all the distinctions of ordinary reality begin to disintegrate. This is Gnostic Christianity; the cross is left behind, below, as we are lifted not into life but above life into a realm of fantasy. At this level the real world is an illusion. I believe that those who begin with a celebration of life, as opposed to those who begin with a dying into life, tend to lose touch with themselves because "suffering is the path of consciousness." [37] If we move right on out into a once-born world of celebration, then life's limitations will crowd in upon us when we return to everyday reality at the end of the party.[38] This is precisely what happened to Walt Whitman. He began with life, but death came upon him to eat out his life in doubt and despair. His resurrection rising is a mixture of adolescent optimism, poetic genius, and a growing despair.

Dying with Walt Whitman

The 1855 edition of *Leaves of Grass* was a painfully disappointing failure, and the continued rejection of his poetry by the public

[35] Miller, *A Critical Guide to Leaves of Grass*, p. 131.
[36] *Complete Poetry and Selected Prose*, p. 293.
[37] Unamuno, *The Tragic Sense of Life*, p. 140.
[38] I believe this is proving true in the modern happenings, whether they are staged in the church, in a huge outdoor amphitheater, or in a sensitivity training center. They tend to become aesthetic productions, and the experience ends with the happening.

was a deathblow to the heart of his hope throughout his life. America was hostile to the creative artist; and during the Civil War, and afterward in the Gilded Age, Whitman's hope for himself and his faith in the future diminished with despair. The robber barons of his day reflected the predatory nature of the average man, and Whitman feared that America was already "a sort of dry and flat Sahara" [39] with no real sense of the community of work, study, celebration, and play it could become. And then there was the tragic breakdown of his health, first in paralysis and then with a terrifying complex of diseases, including the drowning to death that is tuberculosis—a frightening and disheartening experience, especially for one who boasted and gloried in the body electric. These three forms of death—a hostile public, the loss of hope, and poor health—were unavoidable. Add to them Whitman's own loneliness, the poverty of his old age, and, worst of all, a philosophy of life that could not deal adequately with death.

Sometimes Walt Whitman simply tried to deny that dying and death are a permanent part of our experience. He urged us "to pass on (Oh living, always living!) and leave the corpses behind." [40] Sometimes he could do this himself; he would not read Tolstoi's *Confessions* because of their "introspective, sin-seeking" element.[41] Before his illness and the consequences of his literary failure descended upon him, it was possible for him to be buoyant and healthy-minded. In 1856 he boasted to Louisa Alcott that "he had never been sick, nor taken medicine, nor sinned, and so was quite innocent of repentance." [42] In this sense he denied the reality of evil and death, and he tried to live above the limitations of life.

Walt Whitman's more typical reaction to death was to transform its meaning so that he could embrace it as a positive good. Death is "lucky"; death is good in itself; death is a fulfillment of life. It is not just a cruel deprivation of life, but as a "dark mother" and as a "strong deliveress" it bestows a rebirth into life. Life grows out of death. This is not the orthodox Christian understanding of dying into life; rather, it is closer to pantheism and Hinduism in

[39] "Democratic Vistas," in *Walt Whitman Reconsidered*, ed. Chase, p. 163.
[40] Erich Fromm, *The Heart of Man* (New York: Harper, 1964), p. 61.
[41] Matthiessen, *American Renaissance*, p. 591.
[42] Canby, *Walt Whitman*, p. 151.

its loss of individuality to the All. Life and death are part of the rhythmical evolution of the universe, and as "good manure" death is transformed into life through "the leavings of many deaths." [43] He is trying to bring the polarities of life together in a single law: death is the door to life. Death is everywhere and at all times, and it is the ceaseless creator of life. Like leaves of grass life is perpetually transferred from the dead to the living: "O perpetual transfers and promotions." [44] Something of this is deeply real; we all know that we play this role; we are all part of the natural universe. But from the standpoint of a single individual life Walt Whitman was mistaken in making death an ideal. His understanding of death destroys the fundamental Christian hope of escaping Karma's endless cycle of birth, death, and rebirth. It lacks the Christian hope for eternity which John Milton had for Edward King lost in the Irish sea in 1638: "To-morrow to fresh woods, and pastures new." [45]

Many of us are Walt Whitman today. We have lost a vivid sense of the power of evil, we do not know how to use despair creatively, and we lack a sharp definition of the limits of life. Few of us develop a doctrine of original sin, and still fewer fight as though they knew they wrestled with a dark angel. Let us now explore the way in which Herman Melville with his tragic sense of life is a corrective to Whitman's vision of life's natural goodness.

A Vision with a Tragic Sense of Life

America in the early part of the nineteenth century was a paradise for the healthy-minded. Puritanism was dead, Emersonian optimism was rising, and with the opening up of the Mississippi Valley one had only to go in and possess the land. *Leaves of Grass* expressed the once-born enthusiasm of an old culture which had now become young, and Ralph Waldo Emerson was right in recognizing it as "the American Poem." But beneath all this surface a sense of evil continued to exist, and against this frontier romanticism a new realism would arise. For a variety of reasons there were, as there always are, those with a tragic sense of life. Kierkegaard in Denmark, Nietzsche in Germany, Dickens in

---

[43] Miller, *A Critical Guide to Leaves of Grass,* pp. 31-32.
[44] *Ibid.*   [45] Milton, "Lycidas."

England, Dostoyevski in Russia, all wrestled with the deeper dimensions of life. In America, Herman Melville was a surprisingly good secular illustration of William James's twice-born man.

The family was the one great life-shaping institution of the nineteenth century. Tragedy marked the spiritual formation of Melville's early life as thoroughly as did love in the Whitman home. Herman Melville was born in New York City on August 1, 1819. Through his mother's side he was born to the socially prominent Gansevoorts, burghers and patroons for generations, and now brewers and merchants. His father was an importer of French goods, his mother a very proper and proud lady. Together they were petty and pretentious, "monsters," according to Lewis Mumford,[46] all surface and no depth.

In the shallows of this large family, eight children in all, little Herman was a melancholy, sickly child but with a window to the world through the stream of visitors to the family home. There was Uncle Thomas with his French wife, Uncle John who had crossed Russia from the Sea of Okhotsk to St. Petersburg, and of course his father methodically noting down his 643 days at sea. But in 1830 his father's business failed, he sank into bankruptcy, and in 1832, when Herman was only thirteen years old, he died and left his large family to the care of his wife and the Gansevoorts. So at fifteen Herman Melville clerked in a bank, then at sixteen in his brother's hat shop; the following year he taught in a country school, and at eighteen he shipped out as a common sailor on the *Highlander* for Liverpool. As a child and as a youth he knew bitterness and neglect, life was not kind to him, and all his dreams of college and a career collapsed with the death of his father. But from the Gansevoort windows in New York City he had seen the world.

In the tragedy of his early life, but more especially in the over-againstness of the sea, Herman Melville learned to stand by himself in this watery world. What the Mississippi River meant to Mark Twain, the sea, especially his voyage to the South Seas, gave Melville in shaping his sense of self and his imaginative genius.

In his research William James discovered that most twice-born

[46] Mumford, *Herman Melville,* p. 15.

men struggle away from sin rather than toward righteousness,[47] and Melville, like Ishmael in *Moby Dick,* struggled to get clear of all the wreckage of the *isolato,* the isolated man, the Captain Ahab who is beyond the touch of life. First, then, on the *Highlander* he set sail for Liverpool. It was a profane cloister with its own liturgy: pails were buckets, and floors were decks. And it was, as he said, a "miserable dog's life," not just in the work of cleaning chicken coops and pigpens at sea, but in the vulgarity, drunkenness, cruelty, and bestiality of grasping and lecherous men. If possible, the sailors' haunts in Liverpool were worse. But his sailing had begun, and on January 3, 1841, he boarded the whaler *Acushnet* at New Bedford for the South Seas.

This voyage was the great adventure of his life. For one thing it was three years long, almost as long as college, and as Melville later wrote, "a whale ship was my Yale College and my Harvard." [48] The curriculum included a course with a cruel captain, an escape from the ship in the Marquesas, four months with the cannibal Typees, and then with the help of the British, the French, and finally an American man-of-war, a return to Boston in 1844. In this voyage he met dimensions which he would struggle to realize the rest of his life. The natural was one; the natural not just in civilization, but the natural that is really primitive but nonetheless simple and direct. "What's the use of being snivelized?" [49] a sailor asked him. Brutality and cruelty he met too. He was flogged and put in irons for refusing to shave his beard. A frightening brush with death came when with a sudden lurch of the ship he was thrown from the rigging into the water: "And I thought to myself Great God! this is death." [50] Melville returned home with raw experience that would take him a lifetime to assimilate into a solid core of self. Writing about it became his way, as Yeats said of poetry, of "getting the disorder of one's mind in order." [51] In the midst of this process of being born again into both life and death, Melville said that he dated his life from his twenty-fifth birthday.

Writing, with perhaps the most striking natural talent of any

[47] James, *The Varieties of Religious Experience,* p. 171.
[48] Mumford, *Herman Melville,* p. 46. [49] *Ibid.,* p. 48. [50] *Ibid.,* p. 59.
[51] May Sarton, "The Writing of a Poem," *Scripps College Bulletin,* n.d., p. 17.

American writer, now became the way in which the edge of his experience advanced into the depths of life. In *Typee* he wrote a travelogue of his life among the tatooed cannibals. *Omoo* is its sequel, and in these first two books he discovered that he was a writer. In *Mardi,* also a romance of the South Seas, he went deeper and discovered that as a person he was alone, unconventional, and questioning. An *isolato* himself. In *Redburn* he retraced his own life and saw its bitterness; in *White-Jacket* he saw the whole world as a man-of-war, and the malevolence of military life is the major theme. Then in *Moby Dick,* Melville grappled with the philosophical theme that was coming to dominate his life: the death that pride forces upon us in our isolation, and the difficulties of finding a natural way to life in this modern "snivelized" world. In *Pierre* he tells the story of a young idealist destroyed by the myriad conflicts of life. Now the tension between life and death is pulling apart, both in his writing and in his life, and so he turns from these romances to short stories and poetry, and then for some thirty years he ceased to write for the public. He no longer hoped to be a popular author. Finally, at the very end, he wrote *Billy Budd* to salute the great ideas under which he had sailed across a lifetime. His writing had been of a single piece, developing with his experience but with the same essential ideas. With a vivid sense of evil but also with a heart hungering for natural goodness, as puritan in his brutal realism but with a transcendental pietism, he had sailed the seas of despair and claimed a small island of hope.

Herman Melville was a twice-born man, not by any orthodox religious definition, but in the new self which he realized through his tragic sense of life. His religious background, both through his father and his mother, was Calvinist. Although he assailed the cruelty of the old Calvinism, and although he hungered for the new evolutionary love of the Transcendentalist, he never lost the rhetorical no of the Puritan conscience: "For all men who say yes, lie." [52] Evil, he believed, was not just in man's nature, as Hawthorne thought, but in the universe itself. No American surpasses Melville in the recognition of the death and the sense of dying that is rooted in reality. This ugly fact is expressed so beautifully in his own words:

[52] Mumford, *Herman Melville,* p. 152.

> For in tremendous extremities human souls are like drowning
> men; well enough they know they are in peril; well enough
> they know the causes of that peril; nevertheless, the sea is the
> sea, and these drowning men do drown.[53]

And yet there is also life, not a progressive Christian understanding of dying into life, but an acknowledgment that life stands
apart from death and has its own dominion. In *Billy Budd,* completed just before his death, Melville recognized both life *and*
death. An innocent midshipman has inadvertently killed a bully-
ing ship's officer: "Struck dead by an angel of God. Yet the angel
must hang!" [54] Here there is both death and life: "Vere obeys the
law, yet understands the reality of the spirit. Billy instinctively
accepts the captain's duty, and forgives him." [55] It is an image of
both life and death, not the image that Melville wanted, but one
that he found to be true. The innocent do suffer, and someimes a
good man is driven to do things that he hates. And this is particularly true in our man-of-war world in a naval engagement.
Billy Budd, condemned to death, climbs aloft with the rope by
which he must hang himself from the yardarm. Sometimes we are
forced to hang ourselves. Before he leaps he cries out, "God bless
Captain Vere!" And we condemn ourselves as the Captain Veres
of this watery world. But Billy, with the dawn "shot through with
a soft glory as of the fleece of the lamb of God seen in a mystical
vision, . . . Billy ascended; and ascending, took the full rose of the
dawn." This is Melville's vision of life *and* death.

For this some critics call Melville a diabolist, others a skeptic,
still others a humanist, but I agree with F. O. Matthiessen that this
is a profoundly Christian understanding of the problem of good and
evil. It is not the resolution of joy. That is not Melville's spiritual
gift. Nor is it peace. But it is patience, the spiritual gift of patience,
the patience in Paul's great catalog of virtues, a virtue neglected
in our day when we are not encouraged to cultivate endurance in
pain, but a very great gift and perhaps the one spiritual gift possible
for Melville in view of his personality and of the day in which
he lived. He accepted the tragic necessities of life, but he also em-
braced patience, not as a minor form of despair, but as endurance

---

[53] Matthiessen, *American Renaissance,* p. 487.
[54] *Ibid.,* p. 508. [55] *Ibid.,* p. 511.

that could sustain life and then flourish for a brief day in his old age.

Melville's personal life reflected the life of his art, and after the stormy passage of Cape Horn in *Moby Dick* and *Pierre* it was a slow, almost becalmed, uneventful voyage home. He had married the stylish daughter of the Chief Justice of Massachusetts, but little Elizabeth proved a poor housekeeper and a dull wife. The family had four children, and Melville was not much of a father and the children were sour. In this period his life was in his literature, and in aiming for the depths he missed the surface. Sometimes the genius finds it difficult to swim, or even to stay afloat, with his family. His first two books won him an audience; but as his artistry deepened, his audience lessened. His writing could not support the family, and so with a disintegrating art that was weary of the struggle between good and evil, growing debts, a tired wife, ill health with poor eyesight so that he could not read, in addition to the critical rebuff of his books, with all these armadas of misfortune he simply gave up writing for the public in 1866, and became a customs inspector in the "Babylonish brick kiln" of New York City. At first he was a silent, brooding man with a wary reticence, an *isolato* living within himself. And yet he had to go on living; he found life livable, his affection for Lizzie deepened, and he paid his debt to his children by becoming a loving grandfather. And then, when a legacy came to the family just three years before his death, writing became possible again. He wrote *Billy Budd,* one of his finest literary creations, almost as if to show that his imaginative powers were still alive. In his poetry he found peace and a oneness with nature. He had maintained and deepened his life through all his dying.

I see Whitman with all his enthusiasm in a lifelong struggle with death and Melville with all his death and dying gradually coming into the gift of patience.

The Drowning in "Moby Dick"

Drowning, not dying, is the final image of life in *Moby Dick,* but the threat is essentially the same. Dying is always a dimension of life. Melville's greatest sea story moves on other levels too— as a very tall tale, as a salute to the last great days of the whaling industry, as a poetic epic with a marvelous chase sequence—but most deeply it is a parable on the mystery of good and evil. It is a drama of the isolated individual, the new democratic ideal, adrift alone on the seas of life. "Exit the dry, tight, comfortable land: enter wind and weather and sea and whale." [56]

The sea is life, and life is lived in the jaws of death. Evil arises with the good; this is an inscrutable mystery, but it is a fact which we must recognize because evil is part of life. There are demonic energies in the universe, and they harass man everywhere. Captain Ahab represents the individual man; he is modern man, the free and independent individual, the free enterpriser who will go it alone. But he is engulfed with evil when he is possessed in his pride to revolt against the limits of life. He rejects the good, the fellow-feeling that would restore him to the warmth of the human community, and in doing so he becomes an incarnation of evil. Emerson glorified man's will. He declared that if he turned out to be the devil's child, then he would live from the devil.[57] Ahab did just that, and it is not pretty. This individualism can become ruinous in all of us when it leads to alienation from life. It forces us to sit like Queequeg in a submerged boat, holding up a lantern like "an imbecile candle in the heart of that almighty forlorn- ness, . . . the sign and symbol of a man without hope, hopelessly holding up hope in the midst of despair." [58] This is Melville's secular interpretation of the Fall of Man; out of his residual Calvinism he has written of the dying which we all experience in purely secular life. We have traded an open-windowed universe for an egotistical sky. And so, Ahab is the man with a crucifixion in his face, homeless and alone, in the cold arctic wind that was beginning to sweep across the commercial republic.

The answer to drowning is the help of one's fellows; it is faith and the family; it is an enlarged self-reliance which trusts other people too; but it is a life preserver that is not easy to find. It is not something we can find in innocence. In his own life Melville saw that he could not stay with Fayaway and the Typees. In *Moby Dick* there is no answer to evil in the pagan cannibal Queequeg, nor with the Gay Head Indian Tashtego, nor the

---

[56] Mumford, *Herman Melville*, p. 161.
[57] Matthiessen, *American Renaissance*, p. 459.
[58] Melville, *Moby Dick*, p. 178.

"coal-black negro-savage" Daggoo.[59] There is no way back to innocence for a man already burdened with a self-conscious mind. Evil becomes a chronic malady, and no matter where it is checked it bursts upon us from another quarter. Its ambiguous nature is part of the problem. The white whale, for instance, is both good and evil, nourishing and destructive. Moby Dick is blind, brute force, and yet it is Ahab's mad revenge on a dumb brute that gives evil its opportunity. The individual need not be self-seeking and alone. There is dying, but there is also life, life to cling to and to be sought out in the solidarity of human society. Evil may break upon us, but goodness lives and moves and has an evolutionary being in God and in our friends, in Starbuck and in the family back home. Sympathy saves, a divine sympathy and a human sympathy, and Christianity and democracy can be fused together in this natural universe: "Bear me out in it, thou great democratic God." [60]

In *Moby Dick* evil wins; all hands are lost at sea—all but Ishmael, who survives, as if through death, by being buoyed up by a coffin. It need not have happened, but it did. Ahab, but not Starbuck, felt it to be fated. So there is life and there is death, there is good and there is evil. The tension is maintained, not resolved, and the dynamic struggle must continue in his life and in the next book. But, as in Coleridge's definition of the function of art, Melville has brought "the whole soul of man into activity." [61]

Dying with Herman Melville

Herman Melville called his age shallow because of its failure to come to terms with both life and death. This superficiality was true not only of the illiterate frontiersman but of the Boston Transcendentalist as well. By 1830 the intellectual center of the country had moved to the town of Concord just outside of Boston, and there Emerson declared the affirmation of the new age: "In all my lectures I have taught one doctrine, namely the infinitude of the private man." [62] But it was an individualism which broke with all

[59] *Ibid.*, p. 92.   [60] *Ibid.*, p. 90.
[61] Matthiessen, *American Renaissance*, p. 656.
[62] *Journals of Ralph Waldo Emerson* (Boston: Houghton Mifflin, 1904-1914), V, 380.

the institutions of its day. Here, as Henry James bitterly observed, there was "no State in the European sense, . . . no sovereign, no court, no personal loyalty, no aristocracy, no church, no clergy, no castles, nor manors, nor old country houses, . . . nor ivied ruins, . . . no great universities, . . . no literature, no novels, . . . no sporting class—no Epsom nor Ascot!" [63] America was shallow, in short, because there was no synthesis of the contraries of life.

Melville sensed the great polarities of life—"innocence and infamy, spiritual depravity and fair repute." [64] The Latin verb *religo* (with the noun *religio*) means to fix, to fasten, or to bind together, and religion is the way in which we bind life together. Melville had no systematic theology to help him do this. He had a residual Calvinism in his sense of the tragic, but he did not understand how Christianity could sanction and bless a man-of-war. In many ways he was ahead of his age, and so he had to work out his own way of binding together life's contraries:

> In him who would evoke—create,
> Contraries must meet and mate.[65]

In my opinion Melville had the imaginative intuition to sense life's opposites, but his synthesis, the *religio* of his meeting and mating, varied in its success from one layer to "hark ye yet again—the little lower layer." [66]

To read *Moby Dick* or *Billy Budd* is to experience a sharp sense of dying. When Ishmael finds that "it is damp, drizzly November in my soul," [67] we know how he feels. When he declares, "I am quick to perceive a horror," [68] Ishmael speaks for Melville and of the sense of the tragic he would evoke in his reader. This is an intuitive apprehension of the demonic; it is in us, in others, and in the universe; and it cuts deeper than the sky-blue optimism where there are no storms and no shipwrecks. In doubt, despair, disease, disaster, and death Melville wallows in

[63] Henry James, *Hawthorne* (New York: Harper, 1879), pp. 42-43.

[64] From a note in Melville's manuscript of *Billy Budd* as quoted by Matthiessen, *American Renaissance,* p. 512.

[65] Herman Melville in the manuscript draft of "Art," *ibid.,* p. 409.

[66] Richard Chase, ed., *Melville: A Collection of Critical Essays* (Englewood Cliffs, N.J.: Prentice Hall, 1962), p. 74 [67] *Moby Dick,* p. 1.

[68] Matthiessen, *American Renaissance,* p. 436.

"a kind of ecstatic masochism that delights in punishing man, in heaping coals on his head, in drowning him." [69] But, almost as if to heighten the tragedy, he recognizes that it is not fully fated; we bring destruction upon ourselves. Of course, some things are fixed: "This warp seemed necessity." But within life's limits we are free to act: "Here, thought I, with my own hand, I ply my own shuttle and weave my own destiny into these unalterable threads." [70] If there is any comfort, and of course there is, it helps to know that dying is universal and that "the truest of all men was the Man of Sorrows."

Does Melville see dying as the way to life? No, not as a progression which we can consciously create in order to die into life. Rather, he sees dying as the price we pay for our individualism. In this man-of-war world there is no alternative because spiritual health plays a very marginal role in modern life. I would say, then, that dying is seen more as a necessity than as an opportunity. Evil grows and flourishes, as the Bible says, "like a green bay tree" (Ps. 37:35 KJV). It is planted in the midst of life. Melville calls it a necessity, and as a tragic necessity it is not liberating. This static, rather than dynamic, understanding of dying provides a framework but not a floor, limitations but not liberation, for the developing energies of life.

Rising with Herman Melville

In the layers of his experience Melville was typical of the nineteenth century in his affirmation of the goodness of life. The sea is the source of life—that is to say, creation is good. And the individual self, although it may become demonic in its isolation, is still the only way for us to go; but we must cultivate the larger self which we share with all good men everywhere. All this is Emersonian. Whereas Melville was critical of the Transcendentalists' blindness to evil, he was nonetheless in their debt for their interpretation of the goodness in life. Here Emerson achieved a genuine greatness. In their sense of life's natural goodness the Transcendentalists

[69] Alfred Kazin, "Introduction to Moby-Dick," *Melville,* ed. Richard Chase, p. 46.
[70] *Moby Dick,* p. 169.

added their idealistic heights to Melville's tragic depths as the longitude and latitude of his experience.

In the conflict between the generous heart and the ingrown self-consuming mind, life must choose compassion and forgiveness, not the analytical intellect. Melville's hero, therefore, is not the self-willed Ahab, but the tender sympathetic Ishmael. He is the common man; he plays Melville. He is friend to all the races of the world, the whole motley company that sails the *Pequod*. Courage, goodness, fellow-feeling, these are all on board—all the manly virtues that can ride out the relentless rolling of the sea. And behind the actors in the drama at sea is the sympathy of the author. Melville makes sport of no man. Not poor little insane Pip, when the sea had "drowned the infinite of his soul." [71] Herman himself was a sickly child. Neither the cannibal Queequeg: Melville lived among the Typee. Nor Ahab, the *isolato* we could all become, "in all his fatal pride." [72] But this is not Walt Whitman's catalog of virtues with its sympathy for all who walk the city streets, the human tides on Broadway. It is sympathy for lone individuals who stand in the teeth of the storm. "That unsounded ocean you gasp in, is Life; those sharks, your foes; those spades, your friends; and what between sharks and spades you are in a sad pickle and peril, poor lad." [73]

But is there a God? Is there someone to send a favoring wind? The drama of life is not played out in an empty universe, and Melville spoke of "the multitudinous, God-omnipresent" with his "foot upon the treadle of the loom." [74] The critics differ on what he meant. One critic says that Melville was a God-hater;[75] another that he gave up believing in God to become a skeptical humanist;[76] a third finds that God represents for Melville "the totality of human purpose." [77] Perhaps it is safest to stay with what he said and with what he said he wanted to believe. The spirit which he favored was the fullest charity, Paul's description of love which Melville underlined in the thirteenth chapter of I Corinthians, what he called "that unshackled, democratic spirit

---

[71] *Moby Dick*, p. 332. [72] *Ibid.*, p. 415. [73] *Ibid.*, p. 254. [74] *Ibid.*, p. 332.

[75] Lawrance Thompson, *Melville's Quarrel with God*, as quoted by Marius Bewley, "Melville and the Democratic Experience," in *Melville*, ed. Chase, p. 95.

[76] Chase, *Melville*, p. 7. [77] Mumford, *Herman Melville*, p. 185.

of Christianity in all things." [78] Melville wanted to believe that this God must be democratic and kind.

Life *and* death, then, is Melville's message, and the connecting link between his contraries varies according to the layer of the experience. On the simplest level they simply exist together, good and evil, feeding on each other in the mutual devouring of the natural world. As he wrote in his introduction to *Pierre,* "There is evil in the good and good in the evil." [79] Living and writing on this level he wearied of life and despaired of his art.

Melville's deeper intuition, however, was that life comes out of suffering, and we must search for the presence of the good in all these devourings, through all this mixture of good and evil. In his books there is this desperate search. Here he is saying that there must be harmony uniting the yes and the no. There is balance and order, but not a progression. Like Whitman he believed that the universal order should be democratic, but he also feared that democracy might be a monstrous myth. It denies the limits of life, promising everyone equality and freedom. On this level he seemed to believe that good and evil form an ultimate harmony, but he did not see it being realized in nineteenth-century America.

On his deepest level I believe he sensed a way in which death leads to life. The best illustration of this is in *Moby Dick.* A life-buoy was lost from the stern of the ship, and Queequeg's coffin was then caulked and sealed to take its place. When Moby Dick crashed into the *Pequod,* Ishmael survived the wreck "buoyed up by that coffin." [80] It is a symbolic resurrection through which he returns to life. In Melville's own life he found what Richard Chase calls a "quiet heroism," [81] what Henry A. Murray describes as "a position close to Christian resignation," [82] and what I have called the spiritual gift of patience. At the very end, in *Billy Budd,* there is a redeeming radiance. Lewis Mumford catches the keynote: "Not tame and gentle bliss, but disaster, heriocally encountered, is man's true happy ending." [83]

[78] Matthiessen, *American Renaissance,* p. 442.
[79] Chase, *Melville,* p. 111.   [80] *Moby Dick,* p. 462.
[81] Chase, *Melville,* p. 4.   [82] Murray, "In Nomine Diaboli," *ibid.,* p. 74.
[83] Mumford, *Herman Melville,* p. 187.

Harmonizing the Dimensions of the American Dream

Nations are like people; ideally they have a certain unity. And the unity should be rich with the diversity it brings together. In the provincial culture of early America the religion, the *religio* with the binding force, was a conscious commitment. It was Puritan in New England. But in the nineteenth century both Whitman and Melville were left to hammer their own thoughts into unity, partly on their own and partly within the guidelines of their Christian heritage. Both men were richly blessed with a sense of the dimensions of life. Whitman knew this: "I am large, I contain multitudes." So did Melville: "I try everything, I achieve what I can." [84] In reaching for these dimensions they are correctives to each other: Melville filling the emptiness of existence and Whitman cataloging the fullness of life. Both were members of the cult of perfection of that romantic age, and both were searching for a unifying American Dream.

Neither Whitman nor Melville succeeded; neither one became "the focal center" of American literature and thought, but they help us understand the continuing dialogue of our national life. Both men, of course, were alike in so many ways—in the time and place of their birth and then of their death. Both men wrote in free verse; much of Melville's *Moby Dick* can be arranged in this poetic form. But the central point I have made is the way in which they dealt with the American vision of life and death. Richard Chase points out our temptation: "Portentous abstractions and romantic nihilism are great temptations to the American mind when it dwells on the idea of death. Death arouses in us a desire to philosophize." [85] I think that perhaps the reason for this is a tradition of nineteen hundred years of dying into life. It lived on in Whitman and Melville but in a secular form, Whitman as the yea-sayer and Melville saying no. Unfortunately, this heritage was not fully recognized. Whitman more than Melville failed to understand the polarity. But neither one was able to create a conscious progression of dying into life. Jonathan Edwards would be an interesting study in Christian dying, but in general it would be safe to say that America has had no Augustine, no Luther or Pascal, no Dante or Bach in its continuing dialogue.

[84] Chase, *Melville,* p. 53. [85] Chase, *Walt Whitman Reconsidered,* p. 127.

Without the balance of a sophisticated culture it is difficult to create a synthesis of life, and a young frontier country does not produce the great intellectual and artistic pioneers.

In politics and practical life, however, we have those who have been able to harmonize the dimensions of the American Dream. In our common people and in an occasional genius we have had such men. I am thinking of Abraham Lincoln. He had a melancholy sense of the tragic as well as an earthy faith in life's natural goodness. His sense of dying came out of his own suffering. It also came from his faith in Providence: "The Almighty has His own purposes." Humility helped him see that he must not identify Providence with his own cause. This is Christian dying. But he also had a Jeffersonian belief in the mission of the new American nation and in its dedication to democratic self-government. He had a genuine sympathy for the Negro and his "right to put into his mouth the bread that his own hands have earned." Lincoln's greatest gift was to harmonize these dimensions, not as a moral idealist, but as a responsible statesman. Walt Whitman sensed this in the President as their eyes met in the streets of Washington, and Herman Melville called for Lincoln's spirit toward the South in the bitter days of Reconstruction.

The provincial culture that could produce a Lincoln was overwhelmed in the last half of the nineteenth century. Its optimism was not balanced with a tragic sense of life, and America's intellectual leaders almost totally failed to recognize their social responsibility. The Transcendentalist and the abolitionist never really understood that slavery was an institution. It could have been changed, but not with self-righteousness and moral indignation. The polarization between the North and the South could have been avoided if Whitman's idealism had been matched with Melville's realism. In *Slavery,* Stanley M. Elkins shows us that the institution of slavery, here as in Brazil, was a bundle of rights that could have been reshaped.[86] The slaves could have been given the right to marry, the protection of the church, the inviolability of the family, limited vacations, the right to property, training, and education. These things could have been introduced one step at a time, as in Brazilian society, and the institution of slavery could have been

[86] Elkins, *Slavery: A Problem in American Institutional and Intellectual Life* (New York: Grosset & Dunlap, 1963), *passim.*

transformed and abolished. But nineteenth-century America was so implacably individualistic that it had no channels for change, and its culture could not hold its realism and its idealism together.

The Civil War was a turning point in American history; a new cultural synthesis would be needed in the next age. Both Whitman and Melville saw the coming of the new culture; both, despite the rejection of their work by the provincial culture, feared that the new age would have even less heart. War, nationalism, industrialization, commercialism, imperialism, and a large-scale immigration began to transform the essentially rural ideals of small-town America. It is interesting to note the change in our religion. There was a gradual lessening of the religious requirements and a blurring of spiritual distinctions. The lifelong ascetical dying of the Puritan continued to diminish. Next went the mystically rising experience of the Pietist, the conversion crisis and the waiting for the Spirit on the mourners' bench. By the end of the century religion took the form of a business transaction, a decision for Christ with a contract to keep and carry out. The Age of Romanticism was going and gone, and the spirit of the times was ushering in the realism of modern America.

I Am Walt Whitman, I Am Herman Melville

The past is not dead; it is not even past; and we continue to live out of the lives that have shaped our heritage. In the Bible this idea is taken literally. There is a sense of corporate personality in which the past, present, and future members of the tribe live out of each other. Perhaps this is so; something of it must be true. Carl Jung believed that underlying the experience of the individual is the experience of the human race: the collective unconscious. But even if this idea is taken figuratively, it is valuable to see the way in which we live out of the Whitman layer of experience and the Melville. The great experiences, of course, are not limited to our culture. In another culture, say Hindu India, we might trace the expression of dying into life through Siva the destroyer god and Vishnu the preserver, or Siva alone, I am told. There are rough equivalents for most experiences because whatever is true is written into the nature of reality everywhere. But we are Americans, now engaged in creating a new cultural synthesis,

138

and it is helpful to come abreast of the best in our culture and to live out of the heroes of our heritage.

I am Walt Whitman, I live out of a vision of the goodness of life. Most of us do, some more and some less. The Whitman experience opens up to life healthy-minded and happy. I myself, Pierce Johnson, was such a child. I was a once-born child in a good family, and my nickname through junior high school was "Happy." I still find it psychologically impossible to hate anyone. The healthy-minded me doubts the reality of evil. This Whitman experience is diffuse, and it lends itself easily to what was called in Whitman "a sensibility of annihilation," [87] and what I have called annihilation humility. This lacks ego. It is too complete a self-denial. Its core of self is underdeveloped, and it has little instinct for survival. The innocence of this Whitman experience, however, when it is matched with enormous power, can make America a self-righteous menace to the world.

But we are Walt Whitman also in our enormous capacity for entering into life. A negative capability in which there is no judgmental core of self allows us to enter and absorb the world. "Seeing, hearing, feeling, are miracles" and "I can believe a leaf of grass is no less than the journey-work of the stars, . . . And a mouse is miracle enough to stagger sextillions of infidels." [88] We may be diffuse and unformed in our thought, but for this very reason it is easier for us to suspend our judgment and enter into worlds other than our own:

> I do not despise your priests, all time, the world over . . .
> Helping the llama or brahmin as he trims the lamps of idols . . .
> Accepting the Gospels, accepting him that was crucified, knowing assuredly that he is divine,
> To the mass kneeling or the puritan's prayer rising, or sitting patiently in a pew,
> Ranting and frothing in my insane crisis, or waving dead-like till my spirit arouses me.[89]

In this last reference Whitman is thinking of the Methodists in their conversion crises. In this realistic world we need Whitman's

[87] Chase, *Walt Whitman Reconsidered*, p. 126.
[88] *Complete Poetry and Selected Prose*, p. 46.   [89] *Ibid.*, p. 60.

capacity for entering into life. It would be appropriate in "the old hills of Judaea with the beautiful gentle God by my side."

But I am Herman Melville too, and in the terror always imminent and now delivered daily in modern America we must also have a tragic sense of life. The conversion crisis with its mourners' bench can be anywhere today. Five years of personal suffering during high school and college were my Cape Horn. But the sick soul and the divided self were integrated again at 5:30 in the morning on a day in March. Not that life was all settled; not that I could boast of a mystical experience; but I began to pull together as a person and to forge my own identity. This was "my Yale College and my Harvard." But then a new danger appeared, the Ahab syndrome of becoming the lone individual who fights against all natural affection. Proud, now proud of having been broken, and in danger of sinking into a new self, fanatical, perfectionist, and too private for this public world. The master of his own fate and the captain of his own soul is Ahab.

And yet the Melville experience can grow into life in the world too. It must be Ishmael, not Ahab. And there are real advantages in being a self in the world. Yet, it is a dangerous watery world, and we are all physical and metaphysical, and the universal thump of life will hurt. But "the world's a ship on its passage out," [90] and despite the shoals and reefs we have free will at the wheel. The risk is frightening: "It is only in the swift, subtle turns of death that mortals realize the silent, subtle, ever-present perils of life." [91] But with "the rare virtue of a strong individual vitality . . . Oh, man! admire and model thyself after the whale! Do thou, too, remain warm among ice. Do thou, too, live in this world without being of it, . . . [and] like the great whale, retain, O man! in all seasons a temperature of thine own." [92]

Sometimes it seems that we take the worst from Whitman and add it to the worst from Melville. We can so easily become "cynical idealists," idealistic about our own motives and cynical about those of others. Nothing could be worse. But to take Whitman and Melville at their best, we would have joy in singing the song of the Open Road and courage in rounding our own Cape Horn. Nothing could be better for the American Dream.

[90] *Moby Dick*, p. 31. [91] Mumford, *Herman Melville*, p. 170.
[92] *Moby Dick*, p. 244.

6 ✑ *The Dying into Life of a Modern Man*

> The Church knows two lives. . . . The one is in the work of
> action, the other in the reward of contemplation; . . . the one
> is anxious with the care of getting the victory, the other in
> the peace of victory is without care.
> So the one life is loved, the other endured. But the one
> which is endured is more abundantly fertile, so that it becomes
> beloved, if not for its own sake, at any rate for its offspring. . . .
> But the life given up to the pursuit of contemplation desires to
> be free from all business, and therefore is sterile. For by
> striving after leisure, whereby the pursuit of contemplation is
> enkindled, it is not brought into touch with men's infirmities,
> who desire to be helped in their needs. But the contemplative
> life also is aflame with the love of generating, for it desires to
> teach what it knows. Mankind have more appreciation for the
> active life, whereby their infirmities and necessities are cared
> for, than for the contemplative, from which what is divine and
> unchangeable is learned. But those who spend their life in
> active good works . . . will bear witness to that other life.
>
> Augustine[1]

Can we create a life style in our secular society which unites the
work of the world with a deep personal experience of dying into
life? Can we match our critical scientific no with the wonder of
a mystical yes? In this chapter Dag Hammarskjöld's life will be
presented as a self-conscious modern interpretation of the traditional union of the Two Lives.

The Sentence of Death in a Secular Society

Sometime in the sixties a sense of death returned to America.
For some, of course, it never left. There are always those who
recognize the limits of life. But for a variety of reasons the
American culture has for the first time experienced the ultimate
threat to its dream of endless progress, a sentence of death upon

[1] Butler, *Western Mysticism*, pp. 157, 159-60.

everything we value. Terror is not too big a word for what is coming upon us. Death is in the air,[2] and we have almost no way to interpret what is happening in our deteriorating world. For most people religion is no longer a defense, and in the words of the psalmist "the night stalker" outside us and "the midday demon" within are a threat throughout the land (Ps. 91:6).

Can the sense of death become generative in our day? The ancient world was like the modern world in its preoccupation with death, and the apostle Paul turned it to account and made life out of death the central image of the new Christian faith: "We felt that we had received the sentence of death; but that was to make us rely not on ourselves but on God who raises the dead" (II Cor. 1:9). In our day an interpretation of death would need to deal with the intense individualism of modern man. The worst fears of Walt Whitman and Herman Melville have been realized. The commercial republic has destroyed the old provincial culture, and in its place we now have the egotistical sky of the Faustian man who would be his own God. We are "big city hordes" with our "overstimulation, overproduction, overconsumption, over-population and overexpression," [3] but we are more individual than ever, and with a growing sense of isolation and insecurity. We need a new way of dealing with death.

There are many ways in which an individual might hope to come to terms with the threat of death. Some want to go back to an earlier day. Much of the new poetry has a "nostalgia for the lost forests, rivers and prairies, yearning for Indian voices." [4] Others like Dylan Thomas simply scream their opposition: "Rage, rage against the dying of the light." Still others find help in "the novels of Sigmund Freud" and in his "Horatio Alger stories for intellectuals: stories with a message, 'You too can win success in a cruel stupid world.' " [5] Whatever we do will not come easy. The individual in the loneliness of a secular society must learn to live with the sentence of death.

---

[2] Edwin S. Schneidman, "The Enemy," *Psychology Today,* August, 1970, p. 37: "We are probably more death-oriented today than we have been since the days of the Black Plague in the fourteenth century."

[3] Gerald Sykes, *The Hidden Remnant* (New York: Harper, 1962), p. 156.

[4] Jascha Kessler, "New U. S. Poetry: Little Rhyme and Less Reason," *Los Angeles Times,* March 23, 1969, p. 41.

[5] Sykes, *The Hidden Remnant,* p. 52.

In this chapter I will present the life of Dag Hammarskjöld to illustrate the theme of dying into life in the modern world. He was born July 29, 1905, the son of the Swedish prime minister during World War I. On both his father's and his mother's side he was descended from a long line of public servants. He never married. Trained in law and economics, he became a professional civil servant and then, for eight and one half years, the Secretary-General of the United Nations. In his active life he was a great "worldly" success; he had a firm grip on the economic and political realities of the twentieth century. In September of 1961 he died in an air crash in Northern Rhodesia while flying to negotiate a cease-fire between the armed forces of the United Nations and Katanga. At his death a spiritual diary which he had kept for thirty-six years was discovered. In it there is the record of his contemplative life, his spiritual journey across the years, and his commitment to the way of the cross. It is the rare attempt of a modern man to lead what Augustine called "the two lives" of action and contemplation, and a contemporary interpretation of dying and rising with Christ.

A Universal Man in the Twentieth Century

Genuine goodness is never dull, and the Hammarskjöld family was both wonderfully good and yet surprisingly alive to the depths of life. Contrary to what is commonly thought, there can be a poignant suffering quality in a good home as well as in the obviously shattered family. This is true, I think, because life itself is such an unfathomable mystery, and genuine goodness never presumes to have all the answers. Far from it. Often it is precisely the good family in the peaceful and prosperous land, with the favoring wind of a beautiful countryside, which prompts the sharpest self-criticism and the deepest searching of life. Dag Hammarskjöld had all these blessings.

"From generations of soldiers and government officials on my father's side I inherited a belief that no life was more satisfactory than one of selfless service to your country—or humanity." [6]

---

[6] Hammarskjöld, "Old Creeds in a New World," in Henry P. Van Dusen, *Dag Hammarskjöld: The Statesman and His Faith* (New York: Harper, 1967), pp. 46-47.

With these words, part of a credo he wrote in 1953 for Edward R. Murrow's radio program, Dag Hammarskjöld summarized one side of his heritage. In 1610 King Charles IX of Sweden knighted a cavalry captain with the name "hammer shield" and thus raised one of his followers to the civil service aristocracy that the crown was to employ in governing the kingdom. Hjalmar Hammarskjöld, Dag's father, typified the best in a distinguished family. Trained as a scholar, philologist, and professor of civil law, he served Sweden as Minister of Justice, Minister of Education, Minister to Copenhagen, and from 1914 to 1917 as the Prime Minister who successfully maintained Sweden's neutrality in World War I. Both before and after the war, however, he served as the provincial governor of Uppland, and it was largely in the Vasa Castle at Uppsala that his family of four sons were raised. A commanding figure with strong principles and an "obdurate self-sufficiency," a man who could recoup the family fortune from financial insecurity and translate Spanish and Portuguese folk songs, Hjalmar Hammarskjöld represented the strength and sacrifice of service, as Dag wrote, with "an obvious but subtle interdependence between national and family feeling." [7]

"From scholars and clergymen on my mother's side I inherited a belief that, in the very radical sense of the Gospels, all men were equals as children of God." With these words, also taken from his credo for the Edward R. Murrow radio address, Dag Hammarskjöld paid equal tribute to his mother's influence. Agnes Hammarskjöld was gracious, warmhearted, and outgoing in her goodness, and yet intellectual and deeply sensitive. She was always, I believe, the person closest to her son Dag, both in his early years and in their lifelong friendship. She would take Dag, the youngest of her four boys, to church at the Uppsala Cathedral, and together they would visit the poor. Not until he was forty years old did Dag establish his own home apart from his parents, and he never married. So it was lunch at home, and every day Dag would bring his mother flowers. Dinner was at home too, and when Dag lived in Paris, he flew to Stockholm to be home for the weekend. In

[7] Inaugural Address as a member of the Swedish Academy, Stockholm, December 20, 1954, in *Servant of Peace: A Selection of the Speeches and Statements of Dag Hammarskjöld*, ed. Wilder Foote (New York: Harper, 1963), p. 65.

his self-sacrificing career as a civil servant he followed his father, and in the evangelical spirit which we shall discover later in his diary Dag reflected the deeply personal influence of his mother.

In his own life, the credo continues, "the beliefs in which I was once brought up . . . were recognized by me as mine in their right and by my free choice." His father's influence, the ambition and drive, were most apparent at first. He was a brilliant student in the gymnasium and university at Uppsala, and according to a classmate he had "the best examination certificate in 100 years." [8] His major studies were in literature, philosophy, French, and political economy. He completed the B.A. at twenty, the Bachelor of Law at twenty-five, and the Ph.D. at twenty-eight. His interests, of course, were broader than his studies. At twenty he served as an usher at the Universal Christian Conference on Life and Work in Stockholm, and for a time he was attracted by the idea of studying theology. It was in his student days that he first began to read Pascal, at the suggestion, incidently, of Mrs. Söderblom, the wife of the primate of the Church of Sweden, and in thought and style we can see Pascal's influence in Dag's own spiritual diary. Perhaps the point to make is that in an adolescence that matured late he made the best of the best and yet retained a searching intellectual humility almost, as he says, as an "atonement for the guilt you carry because of your good fortune." [9]

Maturity is the word that best expresses his early goal, a maturity with an amazing variety of interests that flowed out of his reverence for life. He was first and last an intellectual; he loved books and he gave them as presents—*Dr. Zhivago* to Krishna Menon, Teilhard de Chardin's *The Phenomenon of Man* to David Ben-Gurion. He was also a translator, and at the time of his death he was translating Saint-John Perse from the French and Martin Buber from the German. He was a poet, and W. H. Auden in his introduction to *Markings* calls his gifts extraordinary.[10] His interest in Eugene O'Neill and his visit to Mrs. O'Neill turned up two new plays not known by the public, *A Long Day's Journey into Night* and *A Touch of the Poet,* and sparked the worldwide

[8] Joseph P. Lash, *Dag Hammarskjöld* (Garden City, N. Y.: Doubleday, 1961), p. 21.

[9] Hammarskjöld, *Markings,* p. 50.

[10] *Ibid.,* p. xi.

revival of O'Neill's plays. His taste in painting centered on the moderns—Braque, Matisse, Picasso. The director of the Museum of Modern Art, after an hour of canvassing their collection for the Secretary-General's office at the UN, asked whether he was "the director of the Swedish Royal Museum." His love of music was for the great classical composers, and in his eight-room apartment on Park Avenue in New York City, he would listen to Bach and Mozart and "of course Beethoven." But his interests were not entirely intellectual. He was an amateur photographer, proud of the pictures he had taken of Mt. Everest on a three-day visit to Nepal. He had the European love for a car speeding at eighty miles an hour. And above all he loved nature, the Swedish countryside and long walks and mountains to climb. He was president of the Swedish Mountaineers' Club, and through his efforts an anthology of nature descriptions, *Swedish Nature,* was published. Judged by these wide-ranging interests Dag Hammarskjöld must surely be seen as an intellectual, and as one with tastes that kept him from the close-quartered intimacy of a settled life.

The mask that Dag Hammarskjöld wore prevented people from seeing the tensions under which he lived. His love of consistency and continuity, his immovable honor—these could be seen and appreciated. He appeared to be a Swedish aristocrat and a self-effacing public servant. To strangers he seemed to be a sensitive but somewhat remote person, always working and always in a hurry. His fellow workers could see beneath the surface and recognize his driving ambition, the very aggressive superego underneath his Swedish formality. Even to his friends, "he was a good fellow, but not one with whom to get intimate." They apparently thought he was too cerebral for women, one too likely "to discuss French literature of the fifteenth century over porridge!" And he was, of course, a most amazing intellectual. When asked what single book he would choose if he were forced to live for a time completely isolated from the world, he answered "Cervantes' *Don Quixote,* if possible in an old French edition." [11] This self-sufficient intellectualism could, on occasion, be rude and outraged and totally rejecting. It must have seemed that he was hiding behind his incessant cigar. He so seldom laughed. All this criticism is

[11] Van Dusen, *Dag Hammarskjöld,* p. 117.

true, and yet only half of the truth. He was, as Voltaire said of Pascal, "the sublime misanthrope." And it is out of all this and against all this that he works and struggles and dies and manages somehow to be open to a deeply personal quality of life.

Dag Hammarskjöld can be seen, then, as representative of the sophisticated, intellectual, sensitive, universal man of today's world and the immediate future. The college professor, the suburban housewife, the government official, the business executive, the modern minister, the world traveler, sophisticated skeptics of every kind—all these can be seen in the image of his interests. Perhaps these are the people who purchased a phenomenal 450,000 copies of *Markings* within six months of its publication, and then, as Henry Van Dusen writes, found this spiritual autobiography "very hard going." [12] Behind the surface of his interests "that other life," as Augustine put it, was also growing, but not as something psychic and magical, but within a career dedicated to service.

Public Servant to the World

Whatever else happened in his life, Dag Hammarskjöld always worked such long hours at his job, day in and out, and in all his work across the years, that his dedication was simply overwhelming. In Stockholm he began the habit of working all day and into the night until five o'clock in the morning, and then he would be back at work again by nine thirty. In periods of crisis he would almost give up sleep; during the Suez crisis he slept two or three hours *all week*. I am not sure what to make of this. It might be called a severe style of asceticism. I think it was. Perhaps it was also a way of escaping life. In any event, his life was shaped by work, by patient perseverance, and by careful attention to detail. Those who wrote him generally received an answer by return mail. Those who sent him a useful clipping might receive a telegram of thanks. It was an outflowing of power, but he was just as creative in the large as he was careful in the small. His whole life was intentional.

Hammarskjöld was a professional civil servant with training in law but with economics as his major interest. His doctoral dissertation was entitled "The Spread of Boom and Depression," and

[12] *Ibid.*, p. ix.

he is credited with coining the term "a planned economy." He was one of the international corps of young economists who built the welfare state during the Great Depression. In 1935 he became Secretary of the National Bank of Sweden; in 1936 he was appointed Under-Secretary of Finance; in 1941 he was named Chairman of the Board of the Swedish National Bank; in 1947 he was Under-Secretary and then Secretary-General of the Foreign Office; and from there he became the head of Sweden's delegation to the Organization for European Economic Cooperation. This is the general route through which his reputation for clarity and compromise won him the nomination as Secretary-General of the United Nations in 1953.

In the eight and one half years in which he was Secretary-General, Dag Hammarskjöld worked out a new and distinctive style of diplomacy. The first crisis came in 1954 with a resolution requesting the Secretary-General to make "continuing and unremitting" efforts for the release of fifteen American airmen held by Communist China. Here and in some seventy-seven other journeys abroad he developed a dynamic role for his office. His approach was through "quiet diplomacy," that is, face-to-face mediation in preference to the "open diplomacy" which could easily degenerate into propaganda. It could also be "preventive diplomacy," especially where the UN was invited to station peacekeeping forces. This, of course, necessitated calculated risks, and Dag himself would fly to the troubled area both as mediator and as executive director of the UN troops. His hope was to establish the presence of the United Nations and to create an international forum as a focus for world opinion.

In developing this strategy, Hammarskjöld also realized that comprehensive changes would have to be effected to prevent these crises from arising. Here he named five objectives that the United Nations should pursue to secure a peaceful world—the peaceful settlement of disputes, the control of the use of force, the rule of law, political equality, and equal economic opportunity. In the long run these general objectives would require the establishment of a world authority, peace-keeping procedures, and agencies for economic and social progress. For these goals he provided strong leadership, and it was his hope that economic and political forces would support the development. In his eight years he won a great

measure of success, even in the Congo, where international cooperation through the UN began to fade with the intensification of
the Cold War. Yet there he prevented the Cold War from spread-
ing, a general African war from beginning, and the Congo's unity
as a nation from being destroyed. But his role as "custodian of the
brush-fire peace" was ending. The successes he won could not
have continued if he had lived, and since his death the failure of the
major powers to work together has prevented the UN from
achieving its peace-keeping purposes. In his policies and in his
objectives, however, he had lined out the directions in which the
world community must move as it organizes not a worldwide uniformity but a way of making the world community safe for
diversity.

Why, then, if Dag Hammarskjöld was such a worldly success in
his active life, did he consider himself such a failure? Never poor,
always healthy, an outstanding success, and yet both as a boy
and as a man he experineced great spirtual distress, a deeply
poignant experience of Christian dying.

His Sickness unto Death

That there was a contemplative life behind his active life was a
surprise to everyone, especially to his closest friends. At his death
his diary was discovered: *Markings,* with its 600 entries over a
period of 36 years, a book of some 221 pages written in the style of
Pascal's *Pensées,* "as a sort of *white book* concerning my ne-
gotiations with myself—and with God." [13] In it there is not one
single reference to his public career, and yet his contemplative
life was not just another life, separate from his work and hidden
deeply within. Dag claimed that *Markings* provided "the only
true 'profile' that can be drawn." This, of course, is an overstate-
ment, but it suggests that his whole life must be interpreted with
its perspective. And the style seen throughout his diary is one of
Christian dying, one in which self-surrender is the way to self-
realization. I believe we have here a most amazing, modern attempt to unite the Two Lives into a style of dying and rising with
Christ.

[13] *Markings,* p. v.

"Death," Hammarskjöld wrote in his diary, "was always one of the party." [14] The form it took in his life was loneliness, a loneliness that amounted to anguish and alienation. It was almost as if a demonic force separated him from life. His friends called him "a lonely man," and one confessed: "I must admit that until I read his book I had never dreamt that his isolation was so horrible a torment." [15] His distaste for both formal and informal occasions was obvious—he called them "the hell of spiritual death." [16] It seems that he unconsciously tried to stay away from human contact. His handshake was weak, and he was so quiet that he was hard to interview. All this he knew; he said the same of himself, confessing in his diary "the anguish of loneliness, . . . the same continual loneliness, . . . the loneliness which is the final lot of all." [17] "Work," he wrote, and undoubtedly thinking of himself, was "an anesthetic against lonliness, books as a substitute for people—!" [18] I do not mean to say that his loneliness was constant throughout his life; later we shall see how he discovered the communion of faith. But loneliness always remained the major form of dying in his experience.

Why was this so? The Swedes are a lonely people, particularly, I imagine, a Swedish aristocrat. A high degree of sophistication and individuation tends to produce anxiety. According to Aristotle, "Men distinguished in philosophy, politics, poetry, or art, appear to be all of a melancholy temperament." It would be simpler to say that our criticism outruns our achievement, and so often the talented person has a narcissistic fascination with himself. As Dag said, "You are your own god." [19] His refusal to give himself in marriage may have driven him toward an ultimate union. As he quoted John of the Cross: "Faith is the union of God with the soul." [20] But his loneliness, and perhaps his failure to find a life partner, left him saying that "my life is worse than death." [21] Fortunately, however, he was able to use his loneliness in a generative way: "Pray that your loneliness may spur you into finding something to live for, great enough to die for." [22]

[14] *Ibid.,* p. 106.

[15] Sven Stolpe, *Dag Hammarskjöld: A Spiritual Portrait* (New York: Scribner's, 1966), p. 114.

[16] *Markings,* p. 62.   [17] *Ibid.,* pp. 38, 49, 58.   [18] *Ibid.,* p. 82.   [19] *Ibid.,* p. 15.   [20] Van Dusen, *Dag Hammarskjöld,* p. 46.   [21] *Markings,* p. 166.   [22] *Ibid.,* p. 85.

In *Markings* we can trace his spiritual progression from loneliness to despair and then on into life again. The earliest notes suggest his search for honesty and maturity, subjects one might expect from a young man in his early twenties. As he began his working career, he wrote down very little, apparently because he was preoccupied with his work. In the next decade, from age thirty-six to forty-six, his interests focused on three major themes—God, death, and "others." His search for identity was reaching out toward the limits of life. In the next three years, from 1950 to 1952, just before his election as Secretary-General of the United Nations, he experienced what John of the Cross called the "dark night of the soul." The legacy of loneliness which he knew as a boy had now become a loneliness "worse than death." In 1950, and then on New Year's Day for the next four years, he began to meditate on death in the words of a Swedish hymn, "Night is drawing nigh." [23] And as he thought of death, he learned to accept death and dying as part of life. With a deliberate asceticism he resolved to try to eliminate his selfishness. Joseph Conrad's *Lord Jim* provided a sympathetic Christ figure for him in this period, almost as if Dag needed to be reassured by its darkness and despair. In the middle of this period, at a time we now know to be when he first undertook the study of Albert Schweitzer's *The Quest of the Historical Jesus,* there is a long entry in *Markings* in which Hammarskjöld meditates on Jesus and "the road of possibility [that] might lead to the Cross." [24] In the dark night his loneliness was being given the depths of dying and the meaning of the cross.

A Knight of Infinite Resignation

"Infinite resignation is the last stage before faith, so that one who has not performed this movement does not possess faith." [25]

With these words Sören Kierkegaard describes what he called resignation, and what Paul called dying, which prepares the way for faith. Although Dag Hammarskjöld did not quote Kierkegaard

---

[23] *Ibid.,* p. 37.   [24] *Ibid.,* p. 68.
[25] Sören Kierkegaard, *Fear and Trembling,* in Walter Lowrie, *Kierkegaard,* p. 266.

in *Markings,* there apparently is something of a Scandinavian vision, one reflected in Ingmar Bergman's films or better yet in Carl Dreyer's insuperable film *Ordet.*[26] And I find it useful to picture Hammarskjöld at this point in his life (1950-1952) as Kierkegaard's knight of infinite resignation.

Very briefly, then, Kierkegaard maintained that suffering is essential to the religious life.[27] Not the suffering due to outer circumstance, because this is coincidental, and certainly not the suffering of self-torture. Masochistic people pay too much attention to themselves. The suffering that is required is the recognition that we are nothing before God, and this is a form of suffering that is not easy to realize. Here "the negative is the sign," [28] the negative as doubt, despair, denial, and dying which are away from immediacy, that is, away from the ordinary egotism of leading our own lives. One must learn to maintain this suffering, this sense of nothingness before God. It never ends, and the knight of infinite resignation must eternally maintain his stance—even though in faith and as a knight of faith his eyes are opened to a second immediacy, a new childlike wonder before the world.

In this period of his life, just before his eyes were opened to the second immediacy, Dag Hammarskjöld was an authentic knight of infinite resignation. In *Markings* he used the words "death," "died," "dying," and "dead" seventy-four times, not counting words symbolic of death such as "end" or "sacrifice." Death, as he wrote, "shall thrust his sword/Into one who is wide awake." [29] He knew that he must "accept death." [30] This means "you have become entirely indifferent to yourself through an absolute assent to your fate." [31] Like Kierkegaard he recognized the temptation to use death for one's own purposes. Hammarskjöld had the Scandinavian fascination with suicide, "the ultimate escape from life." [32] He was also tempted by the self-torture

[26] Carl Dreyer, Denmark's greatest film director, made *Ordet* (*The Word*) in 1955. It is a resurrection film with a relatively modern setting and a fine illustration of the theme of this book. It is the story of a young farmer who was driven insane reading Kierkegaard and who is obsessed with the belief that he is Christ. Through a little girl's faith he works a miracle.

[27] Kierkegaard, *Concluding Unscientific Postscript,* pp. 386-416.

[28] *Ibid.,* p. 414. [29] *Markings,* p. 6. [30] *Ibid.,* p. 13.

[31] *Ibid.,* p. 90. [32] *Ibid.,* p. 86.

of masochism, "the pleasure-tinged death wish." [33] And he steels himself to say that "loneliness is not the sickness unto death." [34] No, dying must be resignation before God and a recognition of that truth.

I would call his resignation and his self-denial a modern form of asceticism. Its intention was to use self-surrender as a way to self-realization. It is asceticism, I believe, and not just despondency, because there is a forward movement. There is hard work and long hours of it; there is a commitment to honesty and integrity; there is a critical self-consciousness; and there is a willingness to use loneliness, however defective, as a spur to the service of others. As forms of asceticism all these may appear quite unlike Benedictine chanting and Carmelite contemplation, but they take us back to the natural self-denial which we found in the apostle Paul. Hair shirts and pebbles in our shoes are perhaps gone, but loneliness and hard work will be with us for a long time. And Dag's commitment "to prepare to die well" [35] is still relevant. And his "Longing—among other things, for the Cross" [36] is poignant and painfully apostolic.

His Yes to Life

At a definite time, we do not know exactly when, there was a turning point, mystical rising took precedence over ascetical dying, and Dag Hammarskjöld was able to say yes to life:

> I don't know Who—or what—put the question, I don't know when it was put. I don't even remember answering. But at some moment I did answer Yes to Someone—or Something— and from that hour I was certain that existence is meaningful and that, therefore, my life, in self-surrender, had a goal.[37]

This notation was written in his diary on Whitsunday, 1961, but the event must have occurred just before the end of the year 1952. Suddenly at this time, for no reason that we know, his mood changed. A strong religious affirmation transformed his de-

[33] *Ibid.*, p. 159. [34] *Ibid.*, p. 87. [35] *Ibid.*, p. 65.
[36] *Ibid.*, p. 55. [37] *Ibid.*, p. 205.

spair and despondency, and at New Year's, 1953, he could accept his life as a gift of God:

> '—Night is drawing nigh—'
> For all that has been—Thanks!
> To all that shall be—Yes! [38]

This new affirmative faith centered on a mystical sense of the presence of God. Not mystical in the sense of being psychic, but mystical in the great tradition of Augustine, as Dom Cuthbert Butler describes him, "uniting in himself . . . the two elements of the mystical experience, the most penetrating intellectual vision into things divine, and a love of God that was a consuming passion." [39] Dag, in the somewhat inhibited religious life of the twentieth century, now knew that his life was in God's hands. "Not I," he wrote in 1953, "but God in me." [40] All but five of his nearly one hundred references to God, and all but one of his references to the mystics, came after this turning point in his life. The absurd, as Kierkegaard called it, had happened, and Dag could now write, "The 'unheard of'—to be in the hands of God." [41] He believed that he was now ready for whatever came, and some three months after this turning point he was elected Secretary-General of the United Nations.

We do not know the immediate occasion of his evangelical conversion, but Hammarskjöld himself has named some of the sources of his inspiration. They are listed in the very carefully prepared radio address which he presented for the Edward R. Murrow program in 1953. First, there is his background—his father's sense of duty and his mother's evangelical love. Albert Schweitzer now inspired him to a synthesis of these two ideals, selfless service and a reverence for life, in his "ethical mysticism." Dag wrote: "The two ideals which dominated my childhood world met me fully harmonized and adjusted to the demands of our world of today in the ethics of Albert Schweitzer, where the ideal of service is

[38] *Ibid.,* p. 89.

[39] Butler, *Western Mysticism,* p. 20. The description of Augustine continues: "He shines as a sun in the firmament, shedding forth at once light and heat in the lustre of his intellect and the warmth of his religious emotion."

[40] *Markings,* p. 90.   [41] *Ibid.,* p. 100.

supported by and supports the basic atttitude of man set forth in the Gospels." [42] Schweitzer and Hammarskjöld met once in Switzerland, and on the journey to Africa when he lost his life, Dag planned to visit the man who was the chief inspiration for his conversion.

How to harmonize the Two Lives, the radio address continued, "I found in the writings of those great medieval mystics for whom 'self-surrender' had become the way to self-realization." Three medieval mystics are named in *Markings:* Meister Eckhart, John of the Cross, and Thomas à Kempis. We know there were others. He gave a book of Jan van Ruysbroek to an agnostic colleague in the Swedish Foreign Office. And Blaise Pascal out of the seventeenth century and Martin Buber in the twentieth performed the same function in training him how to maintain the *via contemplativa* in the *via activa* of the United Nations.

One source of inspiration not listed in his radio address was the Bible, partly because this was assumed but more probably because it was after the turning point in 1952 that the Bible became important to his life. The Gospels and the Psalms are most often quoted or referred to in *Markings.* Paul is not mentioned once, and this is unfortunate because Paul's experience provides the interpretation of Christian dying and rising through which Hammarskjöld was moving. It is also unfortunate that he seems not to have read Schweitzer's study, *The Mysticism of the Apostle Paul.* But behind all the inspiration that prepared the way for his new affirmation of faith, he knew that Jesus was the original source of his new life. Just four months before his death he wrote, "As I continued along the Way, I learned, step by step, word by word, that behind every saying in the Gospels stands *one* man and *one* man's experience." [43]

The word that came to represent his new experience was "yes." Henry Van Dusen suggests that the word may have come from Meister Eckhart "one of the world's great 'Yes-sayers.'" [44] But in any event it becomes the occasional *mantra,* the javelin prayer, the refrain which underscores his acceptance of life. "Yes to God: yes to Fate: yes to yourself." [45] And the sequence is such that "to

[42] Van Dusen, *Dag Hammarskjöld,* p. 47. [43] *Markings,* p. 205.
[44] Van Dusen, *Dag Hammarskjöld,* p. 101. [45] *Markings,* p. 157.

say Yes to life is at one and the same time to say Yes to oneself." [46] It is an invocation of what he has found to be true in his experience, and it is also a venture into the unknown where "you dare your Yes." [47] So it has a variety of meanings, depths, and dimensions, but supporting them all is his new confidence that through us "God gives of Himself to Himself" [48] that God through him is saying yes to life.

A Knight of Faith

"The presence of the infinite" transforms the knight of infinite resignation into the knight of faith.[49] But, asks Kierkegaard, how are we to recognize this transformation? There are no external marks, and we cannot tell whether a man believes in God. There is no way to prove that God is present or not present in "the religion of hidden inwardness" which is now our way, now that the apostles and the monks and the mystics are gone. And yet, somehow, in hidden ways, God is present, and there are those among us, knights of faith, who are "able to transform life's leap into a walk." [50] At a later period Kierkegaard was not sure that "the religion of hidden inwardness" existed at all, but Dag Hammarskjöld in all the hiddenness which only *Markings* has revealed was a Scandinavian knight of faith.

In his diary we have the code that will let us recognize the presence of God in the hidden inwardness of his life. God to him was the Father of our Lord Jesus Christ. Hammarskjöld was a traditionalist:

> Give me a pure heart—that I may see Thee,
> A humble heart—that I may hear Thee,
> A heart of love—that I may serve Thee,
> A heart of faith—that I may abide in Thee.[51]

You must "place yourself daily under God" and *"only* under God." [52] Dag believed that we can meet God in each other, and "one result of 'God's marriage to the Soul' is union with other people." Since "He is wholly in all you meet," [53] Dag also be-

[46] *Ibid.*, p. 92.   [47] *Ibid.*, p. 125.   [48] *Ibid.*, p. 96.
[49] Lowrie, *Kierkegaard*, pp. 267-70.   [50] *Ibid.*, p. 270.
[51] *Markings*, p. 100.   [52] *Ibid.*, p. 110.   [53] *Ibid.*, p. 165.

lieved that we can meet God in nature, as in one of the *haikus* in which he spoke of his own experience:

> Alone in his secret growth
> He found a kinship
> With all growing things.[54]

Without Teilhard's rhapsodic evolutionary theology he created his own expression of the presence of God in creation. He stood in wonder before "the extrahuman in the experience of the greatness of Nature" [55] and "the sacrament of the arctic summer night." [56] Finally, he met God through the writing of poetry in which, as Auden noted in his introduction to *Markings*, "he had at last acquired a serenity of mind for which he had long prayed." [57] "The knights of infinity," Kierkegaard wrote, "are dancers and possess style." [58]

"A Room of Quiet" at the United Nations Building is an ecumenical expression of the hidden inwardness of his faith. "The United Nations," he said, "stands outside—necessarily outside—all confessions, but it is nevertheless an instrument of faith." And so "we are trying to create a Meditation Room where men of all kinds and from all regions of the world would have a place where each could find his own God." In *Markings* we know that he studied the Sufi mystics, he respected the Confucian Way, and he visited a Buddhist shrine in Nepal. As a symbol for an altar he chose a six-and-a-half-ton rectangular block of iron ore, the gift of the King of Sweden, for the center of the room. As he wrote, "Glimmering like ice in a shaft of light, . . . the meeting of the light of the sky and the earth, . . . the stone in the center is the altar to the God of all." In the leaflet for visitors he suggested that the appropriate attitude, as if to underscore his own hidden inwardness, is one of stillness and silence "where only thoughts should speak."

Is there a religion of hidden inwardness for a knight of faith? With W. H. Auden, I believe that Hammarskjöld's hidden inwardness isolated him from strength he needed and from help he could have given. Thus he seldom attended church and apparently felt no need for participation in church life. "I am sorry for his sake,"

---

[54] *Ibid.*, p. 191. [55] *Ibid.*, p. 78. [56] *Ibid.*, p. 79.
[57] *Ibid.*, p. xx. [58] Lowrie, *Kierkegaard*, p. 270.

Auden writes, "because it is precisely the introverted intellectual character who stands most in need of the ecclesiastical routine, both as a discipline and as a refreshment." [59] All during his time in New York City, Reinhold Niebuhr and Paul Tillich were preaching and teaching things Dag Hammarskjöld needed to know. And I, as a student at Union Theological Seminary with a country church at North Salem maybe five miles from where he spent his weekends at his eighty-acre estate and cottage in Brewster, was preaching Kierkegaard on Sunday and would have welcomed someone to share my enthusiasm. But Hammarskjöld had weak ties with the flesh and blood of the Christian intellectual community which he needed and which needed him. And so he, like Kierkegaard, never could join "the countless hosts of happy men [who] exultantly proclaim: God is love." [60] With Kierkegaard he remained a corrective and not a normative Christian; but from his voice too, and particularly from his service to mankind and from his confession in *Markings,* the same word is made audible: God is love.

Self-Surrender Without Self-Destruction

In this section I will appraise Hammarskjöld's life in the light of our theme of "dying into life." Was there too little dying or too much? Did he ever use this image to interpret his own experience?

The answer in *Markings* is that this is perhaps the major way in which Dag would like us to understand the Christian life. Humility, he believed, is the central Christian virtue because "to have humility is to experience reality." [61] He spoke of himself as one who "had been granted . . . a contact with reality, . . . a union in self-surrender without self-destruction." [62] Through his heritage and through his own search he became one who experienced, and who knew that he had experienced, a dying into life. What is new in him is that he believed that this experience must now "necessarily" pass through the world.[63]

Hammarskjöld described his life as a dying, and he spoke of faith as "a dying-unto-self." This, he said, is "the definition of

---

[59] *Markings,* p. xxii. [60] Lowrie, *Kierkegaard,* p. 588.
[61] *Markings,* p. 174. [62] *Ibid.,* p. 110. [63] *Ibid.,* p. 122.

faith." [64] He recognized dying as a useful image—"really 'die' in the evangelical sense" [65]—and he knew from experience "the hardest thing of all—to die *rightly*." [66] And what is the right way to die? It is, as Meister Eckhart wrote, to detach oneself from all outward things,[67] and as Hammarskjöld thought, "to know that in God I am nothing." [68] Hammarskjold's goal was union with God, and to reach it "we must all pass, one by one, through the death of self-effacement." [69] He also believed that anything short of complete self-denial was worthless.[70] In his words and in his experience he adhered closely to the traditional image of Christian dying.

The words on rising are weaker, and yet the experience is vivid at the end. "By thy mercy /Abase me,/ By Thy strictness/ Raise me up." [71] In at least one quotation he personifies "Life as reality." [72] More often than not, however, the dying image is completed with a quality of life:

'—With thee; in faith and courage.'
No—in *self-denial,* faith and courage.[73]

We might say that the spiritual formation of dying into life has taken new and freer expression in the modern world.

The tension in the dying, however, remained the same. He rejected masochistic dying, and dying in which "to educate us, God wishes us to suffer." [74] The purpose of the dying is not to destroy, but to make us free: "God desires our independence— which we attain when, ceasing to strive for it ourselves, we 'fall' back into God." [75] In *Markings* the paradox is maintained: "It is necessary to give all for all," [76] the precise paradox which we noted in John of the Cross.

"Co-inherence" in God is the goal of Hammarskjöld's mysticism. This is a word which is found in three places in *Markings,* but one which suggests that we live and God lives and that we can come together, "in the eternal moment of co-inherence, . . . in a transcendental co-inherence, . . . in His hand every moment

[64] *Ibid.,* p. 106.
[65] Dag Hammarskjöld, a letter to Bo Beskow, November 12, 1955.
[66] *Markings,* p. 82. [67] *Ibid.,* p. 143. [68] *Ibid.,* p. 92.
[69] *Ibid.,* p. 25. [70] *Ibid.,* p. 141. [71] *Ibid.,* p. 217. [72] *Ibid.,* p. 130.
[73] *Ibid.,* p. 137. [74] *Ibid.,* p. 164. [75] *Ibid.,* p. 117. [76] *Ibid.,* p. 122.

has its meaning, its greatness, its glory, its peace, its co-inherence." [77] But it is never such a co-inherence in glory that the cross
is lost. No, as he wrote on Christmas Eve in 1960, "the Cross has
already been raised in Bethlehem." [78] The experience of the cross,
as well as the experience of glory, is always *here* and *now*. "Jesus
will be in agony even to the end of the world," he quotes Pascal on
Good Friday, 1956, just before setting out on a crucial mission
to the Near East. "We must not sleep during that time." [79]

"Sacrifice," I think, becomes for Hammarskjöld a word which
he uses in a way new to us in the modern world. "The ultimate
surrender to the creative act—it is the destiny of some to be
brought to the threshold of this in the act of sacrifice rather than
the sexual act; and they experience a thunderclap of the same
dazzling power." [80] That is, for some people sex is a giving of
oneself, a sacrifice. But Dag stimulates us to wonder if sacrifice
is not the most direct way to life, and the way to enrich life, in
leading us out of ourselves into a co-inherence with creation. In
his own life he was "excited by the thought of a further sacrifice," [81] and here we can read a further enrichment. "Co-inherence" and "sacrifice," two words he used in a peculiarly new way,
are words which echo Augustine: "In sacrifice we inhere in God."

The Road to Holiness Through the World

"In our era," wrote Hammarskjöld, "the road to holiness necessarily passes through the world of action." [82] But in our era the
Two Lives are so separate that it takes a rare pesron to have
an active life and a contemplative life that point in the same
direction. We who have been trained by a skeptical science to say
"No" find it terribly difficult to experience the wonder which allows
the mystic in us to say "Yes."

That Hammarskjöld could speak both as a scientist and mystic
came as a shocking surprise to his Swedish countrymen. A Scandinavian journalist wrote: "What Scandinavian rationalism—and,
frankly, irreligiosity—finds so hard to countenance is that this
utterly sane, cool and intellectual man should turn out to have

---

[77] *Ibid.*, pp. 38, 70, 127. [78] *Ibid.*, p. 198. [79] *Ibid.*, p. 126.
[80] *Ibid.*, p. 166. [81] *Ibid.*, p. 79. [82] *Ibid.*, p. 122.

been a God-obsessed mystic." [83] Modern man has generally assumed that the critical spirit of a scientific consciousness would simply stifle the mystic. But we are beginning to understand that both of the lives are needed. We all covet science's abundance, both for ourselves and for the great majority of the world's people that are hungry and impoverished. But at the same time we cannot submerge our reverence for life in a scientific consciousness that will alienate us from the ecological and spiritual resources which make life possible. To survive today we must learn to live on several levels, to develop both technical skills and spiritual sensitivity, because the road of holiness *necessarily* passes through the world.

The Two Lives must be brought closer together in a new kind of synthesis. Our active life must become sacramental, and the contemplative must learn to find God in the midst of creation. No man in this century stands as a finer synthesis of these two ideals than Albert Schweitzer, and Dag Hammarskjöld must be seen as his student. Nowhere is the service of science more fully harmonized with a reverence for life. The theological basis for this new spirit is being carried forward by the work of such men as Teilhard de Chardin and Alfred North Whitehead. Now, as Kagawa wrote, we can see "the immaterial, immortal God in the world of matter," [84] and in the culture that is coming the scientist and the believer must be able to work out of a unitary vision of reality. I personally believe that in the new panentheism of John B. Cobb, Jr., a theology in which God is seen in and through creation in such a way as to preserve his transcendent unity, a tough-minded approach is developing which can command the respect of both the scientist and the mystic.[85] But this new consciousness will not come automatically; it will not be Charles Reich's simple "Greening of America." [86] The new life of the young people will only be a new expression of an old egotism

[83] Oliver Clausen, *The New York Times Magazine,* June 28, 1964, p. 10.
[84] Toyohiko Kagawa, cited by Hadeshi Kishi, *Christian Century,* December 23, 1970, p. 1536.
[85] John B. Cobb, Jr., *A Christian Natural Theology* (Philadelphia: Westminster Press, 1965).
[86] Reich, *Greening of America: The Coming of a New Consciousness and the Rebirth of a Future* (New York: Random House, 1970).

if it does not undergo the dying of suffering and sacrifice as the way into life.

Dag Hammarskjöld represents a synthesis of the Two Lives for modern man. A clear scientific mind, a distinguished economist, a skilled mediator, and an innovator of international principles which the world community must discover again on the road to peace. But he was also a humble man, penitent before God, disciplined and sacrificial, and possessed by hope and a sense of wonder that brought the world alive for him. And these two lives, although apparently separate on the surface, were fused in a deeply interior faith. His successors will take this spirit into new fields because the road of holiness moves along through a real world, and the challenges change. The contemporary crisis, perhaps more than Dag could have known, is ecological, and his scientific mind and his reverence for life in nature would now take on a better-informed urgency. Would he be hopeful in the present world situation? In the short run I do not know, the international scene never offers a simple hope; but in the long run the answer by which he lived was Yes.

> God does not die on the day when we cease to believe in a personal diety, but we die on the day when our lives cease to be illumined by the steady radiance, renewed daily, of a wonder, the source of which is beyond all reason.[87]

[87] *Markings*, p. 56.

A New Life Style
and a New Altar Call

Rain: and over the thorned, cliff-eaten,
Ridge-broken hem of the east
Dawn slits its murky eye.
Two thousand years. And the Tomb-breaker
Rose from his nightlong ruin,
Up from the raveling darkness,
Rose out of dissolution,
Heaved off that sealing stone, looked out,
Looks out. The faithful follow.
This day the neighboring churches
Clang up the summons. The faithful rise,
Slosh through the drench to the steep ascent,
Eight days back spring foundered,
Shook off the wintry hand, came on,
Comes on, under the downpour,
Splitting its blind-eye buds.
  Brother Antonious, "Rainy Easter" [1]

In this concluding chapter I would like to describe the new Christian life style that is now emerging and to propose a new altar call which the church can create to call the modern man forward through dying into life.

The History of an Experience

First let me summarize the conclusions suggested by this study in the history of many different Christian styles of life.

The Western world has known many forms of an experience that can be described as a dying into life. Jesus is its inspiration, both in his teaching and in the example of his life. The teaching is humility, and his life is one of dying and rising, both while he lived and in his resurrection from the dead. This archetypal experience

---

[1] William Everson (Brother Antoninus), *The Residual Years.* Copyright © 1968 by William Everson. Reprinted by permission of New Directions Publishing Corporation.

is the basic stance of Christian history. But "history is baroque," [2] and in each culture the dying and rising have taken different forms. Old styles prove inadequate, new styles develop, and the shape of the experience changes with the culture. Sacrifice is always the ideal, but in each age the experience of dying into life demands a new form. Mircea Eliade describes these as different ways in which a man can set himself free from nothingness and wedge himself into Being.[3]

Jesus is "the author and finisher" of this faith (Heb. 12:2 KJV), but in him the subjective experience of Christian dying is hidden. The humility of his life is evident, his gentleness is apparent; but scholarship cannot penetrate into his self-consciousness to say how it was achieved. In the temptation in the wilderness, on the road to Jerusalem, in the Garden of Gethsemane, he evidently struggled with himself, but he always emerged with such a complete trust in God that we cannot understand him through his weakness. Even the saints, as they grow in grace, feel that the distance which separates their experience from Jesus grows rather than diminishes. So Jesus, the model of Christian humility, does not give us an autobiographical description of the original experience.

Paul translated Jesus' message into a self-conscious understanding of the Christian faith. He declared that in dying and rising with Christ we enter into Jesus' life, and in the description of his own life he showed us how it worked as an experience. This is the great description of dying into life. More than an experience, its reflects Paul's belief that we *actually* die and rise with Christ. To Paul it is objective reality, and no subsequent expression of this experience can ever match his sense of its reality. His ideas, of course, are developing historical concepts, and one would expect them to change. Unlike Paul we do not personify sin as a being. The world did not end in the apostolic age as he believed it would. But Paul's interpretation of dying into life still stands as the classic understanding of Christian dying. It has an immediacy that is possible only for an apostle. His letters trace the experience

[2] Will and Ariel Durant, *The Lessons of History* (New York: Simon and Schuster, 1968), p. 13.

[3] Mircea Eliade, *Patterns in Comparative Religion* (Cleveland: World Publishing Co., 1970), p. 32.

of dying and rising with all the vitality of a man of the apostolic age. In the long history of this experience new insights have been discovered, but Paul left us free to make these discoveries. He had an amazing ability to observe reality, and what he taught was given not as rules but as a direction for the future.

In medieval Christianity the theme of dying and rising was translated into a series of life styles which helped shape the Catholic culture. The first styles were visible—the martyr, the hermit, and the monk. The martyr, like the apostle, might expect to die and rise into life; but, unlike that of the apostle Paul, the martyr's experience could easily become a distortion of the faith. The monk, on the other hand, created an outward expression of Christian dying in which humility was central. The ideal of Christian humility taught by the monks is still written into Western culture. In time, however, the simplicity of the monk became sterile, and the search for new forms of Christian dying turned inward.

Toward the end of the Middle Ages the scholastic mystics arose to give order and depth to an inner experience of dying and rising with Christ. Their exploration of the inner life, though it may seem narrow and highly specialized, is still our best guide to the inward progression of the Christian experience. A danger accompanying mysticism was the Inquisition. These came together in the late Middle Ages, and they sprang from a common source. If the inner life can be known and organized, then there will be those who can judge us for heresy. But with the rediscovery of Paul in the Protestant Reformation we have a vivid new freedom and a fresh awareness of the transcendent God. Martin Luther's psychological understanding of our motives also makes us more modest in our claims. Today we cannot rebuilt the monastery or erect a mystical ladder of perfection with the premature confidence of the medieval mind. But this criticism must not detract from these very great achievements. In both its outwardness and inwardness medieval Christianity continued the incarnation, and the experience of Christian humility was given a history.

The development of Christian dying and rising took new forms in the Protestant north. Out of Puritanism and Pietism, two of the greatest Protestant forms, John Wesley created for eighteenth-century England a new synthesis with self-denial for the dying and a heartwarming experience for the rising. The Methodist passion for holiness was a comprehensive new creation of many of the earlier styles of the Christian life, and as a new interpretation of apostolic Christianity it brought a dying and rising experience to the common man who lived in the midst of the world. In the next century its Puritan asceticism could not be maintained, and its Pietism, left to flourish as a feeling, became sentimental and lost its disciplined vitality.

The experience of Christian humility created secular forms of expression in nineteenth-century America. Walt Whitman carried forward the enthusiasm of the pietistic romantic spirit, and Herman Melville was driven to develop a tragic sense of life. But their spiritual formation was episodic and individual, and in mid-nineteenth-century America we created no self-conscious style of life which could combine the great polarities of the Christian experience.

Finally, in Dag Hammarskjöld, as in his teacher Albert Schweitzer, an individual shaped a style of life in which the old apostolic dying into life was harmonized with a life of service in a secular society. In seeking to understand his own experience, Hammarskjöld turned to the mystics for guidance, and he created a new and highly individual style of spiritual formation. The dying may have outweighed the rising, as it seems to do in our Good Friday world, but most people were amazed to discover that there was also an experience of Christian rising in the very twentieth-century Secretary-General of the United Nations.

The history of Christian dying could have been traced in many other ways, and one of the most obvious would be in the life of the church itself. The liturgy of the church is a self-offering to God, an ordered sequence in which we die into life in the presence of God in the sanctuary. The way in which the churches diverge in their development illustrates different interpretations of Christian dying. The Greek Orthodox Church, for instance, with the apostolic and oriental emphasis of (let us say) the fifth century, celebrates resurrection rising with a theology of glory. The Roman Catholic Church, on the other hand, with its thirteenth-century crystallization of the Mass, traditionally places its major emphasis on holy dying and a theology of the cross. The architecture of the two churches also reflects their styles of dying and rising. In the

East we have a splendidly colored church as a colony of heaven, an outpost of the eternal in an invasion of time. In the West there is the somber Gothic cathedral with its stone gray interior and the transcendent beauty of its windows suggesting heaven and the eternal life with which responsibility and discipline are rewarded. Each church reflects its interpretation of the great historical theme of Christian dying.

With this history of Christian dying in mind I will now venture to suggest the shape it might take in the modern secular world.

The Life Process Is a Dying and Rising

Life is a continual process of dying and rising, and the Christian is to understand his unique relationship to this process in the life of Jesus. This theme has many interpretations, and a new style will be needed to express this ongoing life process in our world today.

The Christian experience reflects a life process which surrounds us on every side. No image—not darkness and light, not good and evil, not truth and falsehood, not beauty and ugliness—describes reality better than the image of life and death, dying and rising. The woods and the fields were witnesses to the universal theme of the life process long before man had symbols to describe the suffering and the loving and all the creative relationships which are life. It is a vast interconneced process which includes life and pre-life, the nebulae and the nuclei, God and man. It is the whole process of life to which the styles and symbols of Christian dying give expression.

Jesus has a unique relationship to the life process. He does two things. He shows that there is a continuous ongoing life process, and then he empowers this process, giving it an objective quality, so that it can lay a claim upon us in our own lives.

Take this first point. The processes of life are always with us, but that they form a continuous dying and rising process is not immediately apparent. Paul speaks of the grain of wheat, dying and rising in a life cycle as it is sown anew (I Cor. 15:36-37). From Jesus he learned, however, that the man who is a new creature in Christ also dies and rises but with all his individuality intact. That we die and rise through this life is part of the discovery, but that we can carry this dying and rising into eternity is the most amazing revelation. Thus, we all know times of dying and times of rising, but that there is an ongoing life process which can combine and carry these insights forward through both life and death we learn from Jesus.

The second thing that Jesus does is to empower the life process in such a way that it comes to us as a personal invitation to life. This is the point of the parables. To whom will you be a neighbor? And can you, prodigal that you are, come to yourself and accept God's forgiveness? In Jesus, both in his teaching and in the mystery of his presence, we are empowered for the life of the Spirit. In him the life process is made objective so that we are given not just a new insight but an invitation and a promise which carry the gift of life.

The Christian symbol for the life process—the living and dying, the dying and rising—is the cross. It expresses man's lonely suffering and death, his ultimate solitariness. But man is not the only form of life that suffers. In the modern world we are just beginning to learn how much pain there is in nature. Recent experiments suggest that plants have feelings that can be hurt. Man is part of a whole creation, as Paul wrote in Romans, that "groans and travails together in pain" (Rom. 8:22 KJV). God is also part of this suffering and dying process if we can believe that Jesus is our best image of God. What is more amazing is that the cross also represents a resurrection rising in nature, in us, and in God. Jesus makes us conscious of the constant cross that is written into all of life. It is difficult for us to believe that God experiences our dying, and it is difficult for us to believe that we experience his eternal life.

A New Altar Call

Jesus preached the kingdom. He pointed to the inbreaking power of God's kingly reign, and as he did this, he made God present. "To make the reality of God present: this is the essential mystery of Jesus." [4] He wrote no creeds; he baptized no one; his appeal was immediate. He simply said "Follow me," or "Go and sin no

[4] Gunther Bornkamm, *Jesus of Nazareth* (New York: Harper, 1960), p. 62.

more." But the first Christians recognized that this sense of God's immediacy would be lost if the life process was not tied to Jesus. So they created the art forms of the liturgy to carry the believer into the dying and rising life of their Lord. So whereas Jesus preached the kingdom, the church preaches Jesus. The point was to make the life process objective so that it might come upon us as an invitation with an empowering presence. Now they could say, "Your wretched quest for God can end. He has come." [5] The church exists to present this invitation to life.

Throughout its history the church has always shaped an altar call for this invitation into the life of the Spirit. This call has been understood on three levels: the God who calls, the person invited, and the way to respond. Thus, the nineteenth-century revivalist thought of God as a stern judge and a loving father. The person called was a sinner who had violated an accepted code of behavior. And the way forward was to make a rational decision to accept Christ as one's personal Savior. All three—God, man, and the call forward—shape the style of the atlar call.

The new altar call into life will be revolutionary in its openness. Neither God nor the sinner can be so sharply defined as they once were in the old styles of life, and so the burden of the call must lie with the dying and rising which is accepted as the way forward. The God who calls, the person invited, and the way to respond might now be understood like this:

God must now be conceived in new ways in modern thought. John A. T. Robinson called the curtain down on an era when we could think of God "up there" or "out there." [6] Paul Tillich proposed that we replace the images of "height" with those of "depth." The thrust of this thought is essentially negative in order to free us for a new understanding of God. Leslie Dewart ventures to suggest that "God is, rather than a centre of being to which we are drawn, an expansive force which impels persons to go out from and beyond themselves." [7] This image is peculiarly Old Testament. Alfred North Whitehead pioneered in a radically

[5] Carl Michalson in an address at the Claremont, California, United Church of Christ.

[6] Robinson, *Honest to God* (Philadelphia: Westminster Press, 1963), pp. 12-13.

[7] Dewart, *The Future of Belief* (New York: Herder and Herder, 1966), p. 189.

new approach which is surprisingly New Testament. He suggests that we have fashioned God in the image of a ruling caesar, or a ruthless moralist, or the unmoved mover. In all this we need to be de-Hellenized. We could understand God better, he writes, as dwelling in "the tender elements in the world, which slowly and in quietness operate by love." [8] Then Jesus would become, as he always should have been, the best image of God. This line of thinking also does justice to the sense of a universal life process which includes dying and rising. In all this we will do better to be open to God with a minimum of definition, and to let him define himself in our own experience.

This openness, of course, does not mean that the Christian must think of God without any of the guidelines of the past. We are always all but encapsulated in our culture, and the traditional tracks will continue. What we have learned from the Bible and from our churches and from our families cannot be lightly brushed aside. Nor should it be. We will continue to live in all our meanings. But we must now call for a new openness to God. With the minimum of definition that is consistent for us we must now be open to the new image of God which we find in Jesus. And in this sensitivity we can trust that God will define himself in his own way.

Our definition of sin should be just as open as our definition of God. There are personal sins and there are social sins. In today's world we are learning that there are also sins against the environment and sins against beauty. No single sharp definition of sin is possible in our cosmopolitan, secular society. We have lost our group identity, and the common standards that make sharp distinctions possible come hard. Perhaps the core of sinfulness and self-centeredness which is now recognized lies in the simplest of definitions. Sin is pride, self-will; it is the lack of humility and openness. Here, too, it is as if we are driven back behind the church's cultural formulas to see sin, as well as to see God, as Jesus saw. So the publican is a sinner, but above all he is a humble man. Through Jesus we meet sinners for whom no catalog of sins is named. The point to make is that we must be sensitive and tenderhearted before life. Anything else is sinful.

[8] Alfred North Whitehead, *Process and Reality* (New York: Macmillan, 1929), p. 520.

And here too, of course, many of the old definitions will continue. Every age is parasitical of the past, and much of the old sense of sin will continue. That it is wrong to lie and to steal and to murder we all know because of the codes that carry into the present from the past. This is inevitable, and this is right. There must be common standards against which we can be measured, and through which we can become conscious of our sin and the limitations of our lives. But as the old life styles disintegrate in our pluralistic society, we are not yet ready to commit ourselves to the disciplines that will be required for the serious work of spiritual formation. In this time-between, then, we must be especially sensitive, especially unstructured and open in our sense of sin.

This suggests that we can expect to see a wide range of people called forward to the altar of life. Perhaps an open-minded and tenderhearted agnostic is more ready to hear the call than the closed-minded and inflexible church member. Perhaps, standing before the altar rail, we must imagine a literalist who hungers for a sense of the final things, a liberal with a passion for social justice, and an agnostic with deep searching questions of truth. All could be open before the presence of God, and all three waiting together on the mourners' bench.

Where, then, does the definition lie? What shapes our salvation? I have argued that the God who calls must be understood in a new more open way, and I have suggested that the person invited must now be seen simply as a person who is open in seeking the truth. The way in which we respond, the process, this is what shapes our salvation. This means that the altar call must be chiefly defined by the process which it presents as the way forward into life. This is the process of dying and rising. This is the way of the cross. It is always there. There in the wood of the altar, there in the potted plants beside the altar, and there in the living and dying of the preacher himself. And the Christian knows it is there, and there as an empowering process, because of Jesus.

The call forward into life should be a call into a life that is everywhere. God's incarnation in the tender elements of life moves through all creation, and a sense of his presence can become conscious in man. It is a universal process, and yet in man it has a particular shape and style. This means that we can see the resurrection in the spring, not in the Easter Bunny with all his gay innocence, but in the dying and rising of a creation which is groaning in travail for its redemption. In man the dying and rising process can rise to consciousness. He can claim the promise that for him the dying and rising is an ongoing process. It continues through life and through death. And as the life of the cross works its way through his experience it will take concrete form. It is surprising how sharply a tenderhearted person will define his own sense of sin. Few guidelines are needed. And similarly, although we cannot give a modern man a picture of God, he will most amazingly find a definition of his own. Thus it will be chiefly the dying and rising style of life, the way of the cross, in which we will find our best clues to our sense of sin and the presence of God.

How we do our believing will then define *what* we believe. John Ciardi has written a book on poetry entitled *How Does a Poem Mean?* [9] and his point is that *how* a poem develops its meaning is more important than *what* it means. We might say that the modern preacher should call people forward into the dying and rising life process as it is presented in Jesus and as it is represented by the cross. This means that humility is the road to reality. This is the *how,* and the *what* will follow. People will recognize their own sin and the limits of their lives, if only they have this heart of flesh. And God will make himself known if we but preach the life process through which God's tenderness can be known. The important thing we can do is to work the process, the *how,* the life of dying and rising with Jesus.

In this I would advocate a reconciliation of the two great philosophical and religious movements of our century. One is existentialism with its sense of the immediate moment, and the other is process philosophy with its understanding of the ongoing process. We need an evangelical conversion which has both "shining moments" and an "ongoing process." The new synthesis must have the highly personal confrontation of the existentialist and the sense of the life process of the new evolutionary theology.

The old Methodist two-stage altar call gave us one of the best ways to combine the immediate moment and the ongoing

[9] (Boston: Houghton Mifflin, 1959.)

process. Here there was a passionate call forward and then a waiting for the gift of life on the anxious seat. There are many ways of shaping this experience today. The church service will always offer the greatest opportunity. A few people, some young but an increasing number who are older, may wish to create a commune with all the group dedication of the Benedictines. A few Dag Hammarskjölds may elect to follow the solitary way of John of the Cross. For some of us our way will combine many of these different life styles. This is true for me. Christian dying is the depth of my experience, a depth I experience both alone and with others, and a depth that I try to carry into the surface of life where I come alive to creation. In all this there is a common formula.

Evelyn Underhill writes: "The formula of real abandonment is not 'Leave all, so that something may happen, some spiritual reward be gained.' There is a full stop after 'all': the issue is left wholly in the hands of God." [10] We are to gather the wood, and (full stop!) God will send the fire. In shaping this experience today we will all improvise our own spiritual style, but we should do this with the guidance of the great Christian life styles of the past. With Kierkegaard's passion and Whitehead's process I am trying to reinterpret the gospel and to fashion a new invitation to life.

A New Life Style

Humility is the virtue which traditionally expresses the life of dying and rising, and in the modern world a new style of humility is emerging.

A negative reason for its development would be the abuse of power which we have witnessed in this century. There is no doubt that statistically this is the most violent century in history. War and power politics describe our foreign relations, and apathy or violence troubles almost all the major institutions of our country. Our economy is competitive, and although this may make for the greatest efficiency and progress, it defeats nearly everyone with the struggle for success. And for a long time we have been destroying our natural environment. In short, we have not yet

[10] Underhill, *The Mystery of Sacrifice* (London: Longmans, Green, 1948), p. 50.

learned to live in harmony with our neighbors or with nature itself. A protest against this way of life is now in progress. The
question we face is whether the protest will be an abortive rebellion, the continuing protest of apathy and malaise, or the disciplined spiritual formation of a new and more humble style of
life.

We can already recognize some of the features of a new and developing style of humility. The peace movement has been one expression. A. J. Muste of the Fellowship of Reconciliation said that
"there is no way to peace. Peace is the way." The communes, the
life style of some young adults, and a new spirit among the rest of
us is calling for a return to simplicity. Henry Thoreau is one of its
prophets: "Our life is frittered away by detail. Simplify, simplify."
This is leading to a secular emphasis on asceticism: blue jeans,
VWs, and bicycles. For ourselves, for the sake of the world's poor,
and for the natural environment we must learn to consume less,
and to have smaller families. I find Charles Reich's *Greening of
America* and Jean-Francois Revel's *Without Marx or Jesus* simple,
overly optimistic, and with little sense of the discipline and denial
that will be needed to create a new style of life, but they are
prophetic of this movement toward a simpler life. A new style of
humility is definitely emerging.

Will it be Christian? Many of its outward forms are deeply religious—its pacifism and its simplicity. All religions must learn to
cultivate a sense of the sacred in the world of nature. But will it
develop a well-defined, self-conscious experience which includes
both dying and rising? Will there be an ascetic denial ("we have
died"), and will it be matched by new forms of celebration ("we
can hope to rise")? Will it be Pauline?

The elements of the Christian experience are all present in the
vast array of modern experimentation, but there is little conscious
sense of an ongoing process which can deepen our dedication to
God. Thus, there is self-denial and amazing sacrifice. Think again
of the protest movements for social justice. And there is a great
movement to recover a sense of celebration in our society. Think of
the sensitivity training centers and the emphasis on contemporary
worship. But few people practice the hard disciplines found in the
great Christian life styles of the past. Perhaps, in part, this is be-

cause people do not know that there is actually an ongoing experience of dying into life.

The Ecumenical Expression of the Experience

Christians have always worked alongside people of other religions in the creation of new styles of humility, and from them as well as from the study of our own historical styles we can hope for help.

Dying into life is a theme which has been explored by many peoples in many parts of the world. In the initiation ceremonies of primitive man we find rites in which a ritual death is followed by a "rebirth." Myths of dying and rising have been found among the San Juan Capistrano Indians of California, the Ainus of Japan, the Koryaks of Siberia, the aborigines of Australia, and many others.[11] In Hinduism yoga symbolizes death and rebirth, death to ordinary existence and rebirth into a transcendent life. The yogi dreams of "dying into life," and then he makes for himself a "new body" in which immortality and absolute freedom are to be celebrated. In the *satori* of Zen Buddhism, as Suzuki writes, "one seeks and seeks, but cannot find. Then one gives up, and the answer comes by itself." [12] This can also be seen as a description of dying. Islam means "surrender," what we might call death to the individual will. And the Sufi, the esoteric mystics of Islam, stress the need to develop a dual consciousness in which man can participate in the divine consciousness only to the extent that he is conscious of his own nothingness. Certainly this too is a dying into life.

In all these forms of dying and rising there are basic differences and basic similarities. In some there is a Life Force to receive us, whereas in others the self is sucked up into Emptiness. In some the emphasis is on dying, and in others it is on the rising. All these distinctions are terribly important because what we expect helps determine what we can receive. The significant point to make is that all inspiration is good, even if it does form a hierarchy. We have a great deal to learn from other religions about the process of

[11] Eliade, *Patterns of Comparative Religion*, pp. 174-175.
[12] D. T. Suzuki, *The Way of Zen*, as quoted by Hal Bridges, *American Mysticism from William James to Zen* (New York: Harper, 1970), p. 111.

dying and rising. In turn, we might hope to help them clarify the expression of this experience in their heritage.

What we learn from other religions and what they learn from Christianity, however, must be given the consistency of a continuous experience. The dying is to lead into life. If it is true that all the world's great religions have a road to God, it would also be true to say that any one section of the road may take us nowhere. The person who picks and pieces from what he likes may have no road at all, no consecutive experience of dying and rising.

In Christianity, however, dying into life will always be more than an experience and more than a style of spiritual formation. It can be, as it was with the apostle Paul, a way of invoking the life of our Lord. His life in us is a struggling with life and death. And as we enter into the lives of others, we shall discover not innocence but a quality of life that has struggled with death. And so dying and rising we walk the way, sometimes rising above the dying, sometimes dying but hoping that the rising will come. But always, in both life and death, we walk in the promise that Christ himself is dramatically present: "All the way to heaven is heaven because He said, 'I am the Way.' " [13]

[13] Catherine of Siena.